Miracle-Gro®

Vegetables

How to grow fresh, delicious vegetables

Table of Contents

D0953901

Meredith® Books
Des Moines, Iowa

Miracle-Gro Basics – Vegetables
Writer: Megan McConnell Hughes
Editor: Marilyn Rogers
Contributing Designer: Studio G Design
Copy Chief: Terri Fredrickson
Publishing Operations Manager: Karen Schirm
Senior Editor, Asset and Information Manager: Phillip Morgan
Edit and Design Production Coordinator: Mary Lee Gavin
Editorial Assistant: Kathleen Stevens
Book Production Managers: Pam Kvitne, Marjorie J. Schenkelberg, Rick von Holdt, Mark Weaver
Contributing Copy Editor: Sara Oliver Watson
Contributing Proofreaders: Terri Krueger, Stephanie Petersen
Contributing Photographers: Bill Beatty/Wild & Natural: 47B; Rob Cardillo: 83T; David
    Cavagnaro: 26TR, 30CR, 30BR, 34, 35corner, 38CR, 38BR, 40TR, 40CR, 40BR, 44TR,
    46CR, 46BR, 48TR, 48BR, 54, 55corner, 55T, 55BC, 55B, 58BR, 62TR, 62BR, 63T, 63B,
    64CR, 64BR, 72TR, 72BR, 74TR, 74CR, 74BR, 76TR, 76CR, 78TR, 80TR, 80BR, 81B,
    90TR, 90BR; Flora Graphics: 55TC; Suzie Gibbons/Garden Picture Library: 52BR; Michael
    Howes/Garden Picture Library: 52TR; Jerry Pavia: 26BR, 44CR, 44BR, 62L, 63corner, 64TR,
    72L, 72CR, 76L, 77corner, 78L, 78CR, 78BR, 79corner, 80CR, 81C; Michael Thompson:
    46TR
Contributing Photo Researcher: Susan Ferguson
Contributing Photo Stylist: Diane Witosky
Indexer: Elizabeth T. Parson
Special thanks to: Janet Anderson, Mary Irene Swartz

Meredith® Books
Executive Director, Editorial: Gregory H. Kayko
Executive Director, Design: Matt Strelecki
Managing Editor: Amy Tincher-Durik
Executive Editor/Group Manager: Benjamin W. Allen
Senior Associate Design Director: Ken Carlson
Marketing Product Manager: Isaac Petersen

Publisher and Editor in Chief: James D. Blume
Editorial Director: Linda Raglan Cunningham
Executive Director, New Business Development: Todd M. Davis
Executive Director, Sales: Ken Zagor
Director, Operations: George A. Susral
Director, Production: Douglas M. Johnston
Director, Marketing: Amy Nichols
Business Director: Jim Leonard

Vice President and General Manager: Douglas J. Guendel

Meredith Publishing Group
President: Jack Griffin
Executive Vice President: Bob Mate

Meredith Corporation
Chairman and Chief Executive Officer: William T. Kerr
President and Chief Operating Officer: Stephen M. Lacy

In Memoriam: E.T. Meredith III (1933-2003)

All of us at Meredith® Books are dedicated to providing you with information and ideas to
enhance your home and garden. We welcome your comments and suggestions. Write to us at:
Meredith Books, Garden Editorial Department, 1716 Locust St., Des Moines, IA 50309-3023.

If you would like more information on other Miracle-Gro products, call 800/225-2883 or visit us
at: www.miraclegro.com

Note to the Readers: Due to differing conditions, tools, and individual skills, Meredith
Corporation assumes no responsibility for any damages, injuries suffered, or losses incurred as a
result of following the information published in this book. Before beginning any project, review the
instructions carefully, and if any doubts or questions remain, consult local experts or authorities.

Fresh from the Garden

Fresh is best! Here's one of many reasons why. A fresh-picked, vine-ripened tomato has up to three times the vitamin C of a supermarket tomato, and the flavor is so rich and delicious it's hard to believe that the two are related. Ultimate freshness and fabulous flavor are at your fingertips in a home vegetable garden. When the distance from the garden to the table is mere feet, you'll enjoy just-harvested, nutrient-packed produce that is superior to any store-bought counterpart because it is so fresh.

A well-stocked vegetable garden doesn't require a huge planting patch. In fact, you can grow a great selection of vegetables in containers on a sunny deck or patio. Dedicate a few minutes a day to weeding, watering, and harvesting vegetables and you'll enjoy weeks of good-for-you treats.

< 3 >

HOW TO USE THIS BOOK

Plant Selection Guide

Flip to the Gallery of Vegetables beginning on page 21 to learn about growing more than 30 different vegetables. Each plant summary includes several recommended varieties and helpful growing tips.

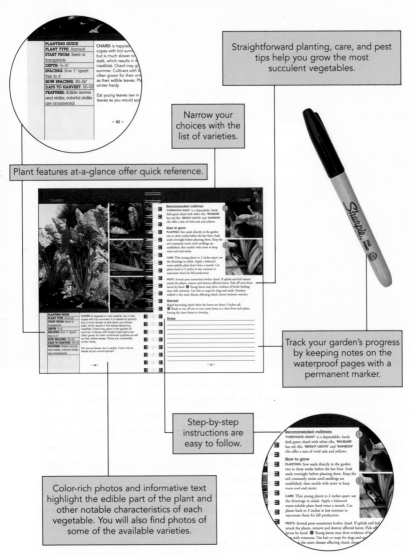

Straightforward planting, care, and pest tips help you grow the most succulent vegetables.

Narrow your choices with the list of varieties.

Plant features at-a-glance offer quick reference.

Track your garden's progress by keeping notes on the waterproof pages with a permanent marker.

Step-by-step instructions are easy to follow.

Color-rich photos and informative text highlight the edible part of the plant and other notable characteristics of each vegetable. You will also find photos of some of the available varieties.

< 4 >

Vegetables are an easy-to-please lot. They grow with gusto on apartment balconies, ripen happily when mixed with flowers in beds of annuals and perennials, and turn out mouthwatering produce in traditional backyard gardens.

A successful vegetable garden begins with a good planting site. Although vegetables are adaptable to diverse growing situations, they thrive in the following conditions.

① SUNLIGHT: Most vegetables need full sun, which means a daily dose of at least six hours of direct sun. Tomatoes, corn, cucumbers, melons, and potatoes flower and fruit best when they receive sunlight for more than six hours, while salad greens, broccoli, chard, and cabbage can grow well with only four to six hours of direct sunlight.

② A LEVEL SITE: Ground that is relatively level is easy to work. Gentle slopes are also good because the soil drains well.

③ DRAINAGE: Soil in a vegetable garden should drain freely. Standing water or persistently soggy soil will inhibit growth and eventually drown plants. You can improve poorly draining soil by incorporating compost into it. Or you can create raised beds. Building a 6- to 12-inch-tall frame and filling it with good quality topsoil will raise the root system above the poorly drained native soil.

For convenience, site a vegetable garden close to the kitchen door. Running out at dinnertime to harvest some parsley or one more tomato for the salad will be a cinch. You'll also find it's handy to locate the garden near a shed or garage where tools can be stored. A nearby water source will make occasional watering chores a snap.

< 6 >

Traditional vegetable gardens are planted in straight rows to make tilling, hoeing, and harvesting a breeze. They're functional spaces and they look it. Plant them in an out-of-the-way space in the landscape so they are not an eyesore. ❹ If you select a planting site that is visible from a living area, there are many ways to make the garden eye-pleasing. For example, surround it with a tidy picket fence, install brick paths between raised beds, or mix in flowers for color.

If space is limited, plant vegetables in containers. Bush or patio tomatoes, peppers, eggplant, and lettuce are good crops for container gardens. Grow lettuce in 6- to 10-inch-diameter pots; containers holding 5 to 15 gallons of soil are best for larger plants. Be sure the pots have adequate drainage holes to allow excess water to escape. Fill the containers with Miracle-Gro Potting Mix and plant seeds or transplants.

< 7 >

Vegetables thrive and taste better if they grow in good soil. The best soil for vegetable gardening is loose, crumbly, and dark, which means the soil has plenty of organic matter. Good soil for vegetable gardens contains necessary nutrients for plant growth and is free of weed seeds and pesticide residue. If your garden plot is not blessed with great soil, don't worry. As you prepare for planting, you can improve the soil.

Fall is the ideal time to prepare garden soil. Extended dry spells this time of year make the soil easy to turn over. Plus, when you amend the soil in fall, the earthworms and microorganisms in the soil have time to process the organic matter you add, so that its nutrients are available to plants by springtime.

If you don't get a chance to work the soil in fall, prepare it anytime it is dry and crumbly. Soil preparation requires time, labor, and monetary investment, but it pays dividends in bushels of flavorful vegetables. Prepare your planting area with these simple steps.

Determine the size and shape of the garden. If this is your first garden, it is best to start small. The largest size recommended for a first vegetable garden is 25 by 25 feet—625 square feet. With careful planning, a garden this size can keep four people supplied with loads of salad makings, herbs, and vegetables.

Once you determine the size of your garden, design the shape of the space. Traditional row-crop gardens are rectangular. If you want a more decorative garden, shape it with gentle sweeping curves. ❶ Outline the bed with markers or a garden hose. Once you are happy with the shape, mark it with sand, flour, or landscapers paint, then remove the hose.

❷ Remove sod and weeds. If you are making the garden in a spot that is currently lawn, use

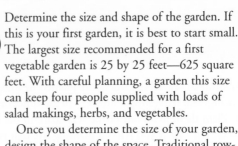

< 8 >

a sharp spade to strip the grass off of the area. Use the sod elsewhere or compost it. If you are removing sod from a large area, consider renting a power sod cutter.

3 Spread 4 inches of organic material over the bed. Use Miracle-Gro Garden Soil, decomposed bark chips or manure, compost, leaf mold, sphagnum peat moss, or a combination of these materials. Organic matter improves drainage and air circulation in the soil, while boosting its nutrient content. Vegetables will utilize these valuable nutrients as they grow.

4 Use a rotary tiller to churn it all into the soil. Owning a tiller is not necessary; garden centers and hardware stores rent rotary tillers at reasonable rates. Tillers with large wheels are the easiest to operate. If the soil is heavy and hard to dig, rent the largest tiller you can find. The weight and power make the job easier.

Once the garden spot is bare, water the area and then let it rest for a few days. Treat any weeds that pop up with Roundup Weed & Grass Killer. Roundup breaks down in the soil in a few days and has no effect on the vegetables to follow. Repeat the process in 10 days to kill any new weeds that germinate. Wait another 10 days to see whether you need to spray again.

5 Prepare the seed or transplant bed. Rake the area smooth and discard any rocks, sticks, clods, or other debris. Spread plant food according to label directions. Use a continuous release or organic formulation to last all summer. Rake the plant food into the soil and water it in, and you're ready to plant.

< 9 >

The plants for your vegetable garden start either as seeds you sow yourself—inside or in the garden—or as transplants that you buy. Garden centers and mail order companies boast a diverse selection of seeds and seedlings. Growing vegetable transplants at home from seed is an economical choice, but you must be willing to provide regular care to ensure the small plants thrive.

Starting vegetables from seed is an excellent option if you would like to grow a particular variety or heirloom that is not sold as a transplant. Some vegetables, such as corn, beans, peas, and lettuce, are so simple to sow directly into the garden that you rarely find them as transplants. Many others, such as artichoke, celery, eggplant, pepper, and tomato, need a long growing season to mature. Usually nurseries offer these vegetables as transplants, but you can also start your own transplants at home. Sow them indoors in late winter and move them into the garden in late spring.

Seed packets clearly explain when and how to plant for your particular area of the country. Grow your own transplants with these tips.

❶ CONTAINERS: Nearly any container, from peat pots to egg cartons, can be used for sowing seed. The only requirement is that water can drain out of the pot.

❷ SOIL: Seed-starting soil mix, such as Miracle-Gro Seed Starting Potting Mix, is best for starting seedlings.

SOWING: Fill containers with moist soil mix, water well, and let drain. Plant seeds as recommended on the seed packet.

❸ WATERING: Water seeds and seedlings delicately with a slow stream of water or by misting them. Keep the soil moist.

< 10 >

LIGHT AND HEAT: Seedlings need plenty of light  to develop into strong plants, and a sunny windowsill doesn't provide enough. Growing seedlings on a light stand equipped with fluorescent grow lamps is the best way to meet your seedlings' needs. Adjust the lamps so they are 2 inches above the plants, raising the lamps as the plants grow. Keep the lights on for 12 to 14 hours per day.

Most vegetables will sprout at room temperature (about 70°F), but some plants, such as peppers, cabbages, and tomatoes, will germinate much faster if given slightly warmer temperatures. To increase warmth, place the containers on a heating pad set on its lowest temperature. Shut off the pad at night. Keep seeds moist, warm, and exposed to adequate light until they germinate. Seeds will germinate in a few days to a few weeks, depending on the plant species.

❹ **THINNING:** Seedlings typically first unfold two small, delicate leaves, called seed leaves. The next leaves to appear are the "true" leaves. These are usually larger and have a different shape. When plants are about 1 inch tall and before the first true leaves develop, remove all but the strongest seedlings in the pot. You can pull out the excess plants or pinch or clip off the stems at soil level.

FEEDING: Feed seedlings when the first true leaves have formed. Use a water-soluble plant food diluted with twice the amount of water recommended. Feed seedlings every 7 to 10 days.

❺ **HARDENING OFF:** Prepare seedlings for the outdoors by hardening them off. During this phase, you toughen up seedlings by exposing them to cooler temperatures, letting their soil dry so they wilt slightly, and giving them more light. An easy way to harden off seedlings is to set them outside in mild weather for two or three weeks before planting them in the garden. Keep the seedlings out of strong wind and bring them indoors if frost is expected.

< 11 >

Vegetables fall into two groups—warm-season and cool-season crops—and you need to know which group a vegetable is in so that you plant it in the garden at the right time.

Cool-season crops, such as lettuce and cabbage, thrive when temperatures range between 40°F and 75°F. In most areas, plant cool-season crops two to four weeks before the last average spring frost date. They will stop producing in early summer when the weather warms.

Warm-season vegetables, such as tomatoes, peppers, and corn, are killed by frost and don't germinate or perform well when temperatures fall below 50°F. Plant warm-season crops in the garden after the last chance of frost has passed. See the list of warm- and cool-season crops on page 13.

Planting

1 Once the time is right for planting outdoors, make sure the soil is ready. It should be neither too wet nor too dry. Press a handful of soil in your fist; if it crumbles, the soil is ready. Before planting, loosen the soil by tilling or turning it with a long-handled garden fork. Smooth over the bed with a rake, breaking up large clods and making sure the soil surface is finely textured.

Sowing seeds

2 Begin by digging a shallow furrow with a hoe or trowel. Drop seeds into the furrow, placing them as close together as recommended on the seed packet. Cover small seeds such as lettuce and carrots with a scant ¼ inch of soil; cover larger seeds such as corn and beans with an inch or more or simply press them into the ground. Check the seed-packet recommendations for planting depth.

Gently water the garden as soon as seeds are sown; soil should be moist but not wet. Some seeds germinate in a few days while others take three weeks or more to send up shoots.

< 12 >

❸ When seedlings reach 1 to 2 inches in height, thin them to the spacing recommended on the seed packet.

Establishing transplants

If buying transplants, select young, healthy seedlings with strong stems and vivid green foliage. To plant, gently loosen pot-bound roots—the ones tightly encircling the root ball—so they don't continue to grow around themselves. Then plant at the same depth as the seedling grew in the pot.

Plant tomato and broccoli seedlings deeper so they don't flop over. They'll actually grow roots on the buried stem, which helps stabilize them. Water well.

Extend the season

❹ The sooner you get plants into the garden the better they will grow and the sooner they will produce fruit. Cold weather and soil often inhibit early outdoor planting. Get a jump-start on the season by using bottom-less, gallon-size plastic milk jugs to make mini greenhouses. Be sure to remove the jugs when temperatures rise above 50°F; otherwise the plants might "cook" underneath. Cold frames, plastic tunnels, and row covers also work to warm soil for good plant growth.

Warm-season crops	Cool-season crops
SOW IN WARM SOIL:	**SOW IN COOL SOIL:**
Beans	Arugula
Cantaloupe	Beet
Corn	Broccoli
Cucumber	Cabbage
Okra	Carrot
Pumpkin	Chard
Squash	Kohlrabi
Watermelon	Lettuce
	Onion
TRANSPLANT TO GARDEN IN LATE SPRING:	Parsnip
	Peas
Artichoke	Potato
Eggplant	Radish
Pepper	Spinach
Tomato	

Garden Care

To reach their fullest potential, vegetables have to grow as quickly as possible. Anything that slows growth decreases the size and the quality of the produce, as well as the yield. Regular watering, feeding, and other care give plants the oomph they need to grow quickly and produce a tasty, bountiful harvest.

Watering

Water is most important for taste and yield. Give vegetables all the water they want and don't let them go through periods of drought. The most critical time to water is right after seeds are sown or seedlings planted. Without moisture, seeds will not germinate. And a transplant plunked down into dry soil droops very quickly. Water a just-seeded bed with a fine shower of water right after planting, then as needed to maintain a moist but not wet seedbed. Water transplants immediately after planting and continue as needed to create moist but not waterlogged soil.

As plants grow, water as needed based on the feel of the soil an inch or so under the surface. When it feels cool and damp to the touch, but doesn't moisten your finger, it's time to water; if it wets or muddies your finger, it's too soon to water; if it feels dry, you've waited too long.

Each time you water, let the hose run until the soil is wet a foot below the surface. To determine whether you've applied enough water without digging, set soup cans around the garden to measure the amount of water you're applying. For average soils, an inch of water in the can equals 12 inches deep in the soil. Clay soils might need 2 inches, and sandy soils only half an inch.

< 14 >

❶ Soaker hoses, with small holes that slowly emit water, are an efficient and effective way to water a vegetable garden. Avoid overhead watering methods, such as sprinklers and watering cans, which wet foliage and promote disease growth.

Feeding

Vegetables have a voracious appetite for nutrients. In fact, vegetables require more nutrients than any other plants in the garden.

Different plant foods are applied in different ways. Follow the directions on the box or bag for application and timing.

❷ Watch your plants. If growth slows or the oldest leaves begin to turn yellow, give a quick feeding of liquid plant food on the leaves and the soil. Another way to give plants a quick boost is to side-dress them with a quick-release granular plant food. **❸** Scratch the food into the base of the plant or along the row. Then water it in to prevent burning.

FEEDING TIPS: Get transplants off to a growing start in the garden with the following formula. At planting time mix Osmocote Smart-Release Plant Food in the planting holes as directed on the package. This plant food will slowly release valuable nutrients throughout the growing season. After planting the transplants feed them with Miracle-Gro All Purpose fertilizer for a quick nutrient boost. Follow-up with another application of Miracle-Gro All Purpose fertilizer two weeks later.

Vegetables in containers need more food than those in the ground. A regular liquid-feeding schedule works well with them. An excellent way to feed vegetables in dry climates is to add some plant food to the irrigation water. Add one-fourth the recommended rate every time you water. Water after feeding to dissolve the plant food and carry it into the root zone. You can take care of both by using a water-soluble plant food that feeds as you water.

Weed Control

Weeds compete with vegetables for water, sun, and soil nutrients. If you ignore the weeds, they will reduce your harvest. Attack weeds before they grow large. Use one or, better still, a combination of the following methods to defeat weeds in your garden.

continued on page 16>>

< 15 >

1 **MULCH:** Mulch smothers weed seeds and makes weeds easier to pull if they do germinate and grow. Spread a 2-inch layer of organic mulch, such as straw, grass clippings, compost, or shredded leaves, around plants. Synthetic mulches, such as plastic mulch—available in several colors—and fiber weed cloth, are also good at suppressing pesky weeds.

2 **HOEING:** If you don't mulch, hoeing and cultivating the soil is another way to control weeds. Hoeing also loosens any crust that forms on soil, which can prevent water from entering and filtering down to the plant roots. Work only the top inch of soil, hoeing lightly every few days.

HAND WEEDING: Weeds are easiest to remove from moist earth, so hand weed after rain or watering. Pull the weed out by its roots. Use a trowel or dandelion digger to eradicate weeds with long taproots.

3 **HERBICIDES:** Most herbicides are formulated to kill specific types of plants. When buying, read the label to make sure the product can be used safely on your crops. Apply herbicides with care to avoid damaging plants or the environment. Weed preventers, such as Miracle-Gro Garden Weed Preventer, are formulated to keep weeds from germinating then growing in your garden. They work best if they are applied early in the season. Before using a weed preventer, remove any weeds that have broken through the soil.

Harvest

4 Vegetables are best when picked when flavor is at its peak. This means harvesting the crops when they are ready and not leaving fruit on the plant too long. Cucumbers, for example,

< 16 >

become coarse and full of seeds if not picked promptly. Also, harvesting vegetables is like picking flowers; the plants stop producing if the crops are not harvested.

Seed packets and plant catalogs usually list "days to harvest" to give you an idea of when the crop will be ready to pick. Some crops, such as radishes, are ready for harvest in 25 to 30 days; other crops take 90 days or more to mature.

Take note of the days to harvest for your crops and time planting in your garden accordingly. For example, if you will be away from your garden for two weeks in August, expedite or delay planting vegetables so that they fruit before you leave or after you return. By doing this you'll enjoy all the fruit of your labor at its peak.

For harvesting purposes, vegetable crops can be divided into three categories: those that should be harvested as soon as they are ripe, those that can wait a few days, and those that can wait a few weeks. For ultimate flavor, pick vegetables as recommended below.

HARVEST AS SOON AS THEY RIPEN: beans, corn, cucumbers, and peas.
HARVEST WITHIN A FEW DAYS AFTER RIPENING: broccoli, cabbage, lettuce, radishes, summer squash, tomatoes, and zucchini.
CAN LEAVE IN THE GARDEN FOR SEVERAL WEEKS: beets and other root vegetables, carrots, kale, leeks, pumpkins, winter squash.

< 17 >

Problem Solving

Sometimes, in spite of our best efforts, things go wrong. Weeds, pests, diseases, or environmental problems, such as too little light or too much water, plague crops and reduce harvest.

Your first line of defense is prevention. Grow healthy plants. Vegetables that are well established and healthy are better able to fight off pests and diseases than are weak or sick plants. Regular watering and feeding go a long way to growing strong plants and a bountiful crop.

Next, select naturally pest-resistant varieties. Numerous vegetable varieties are resistant to specific problems. For example, the ears of some corn cultivars are so tightly wrapped in the husk that corn earworms can't reach them. Some tomato varieties resist a range of diseases.

Finally, if you know that a particular pest is an ongoing and serious problem in your area, either search for resistant varieties or don't grow that vegetable at all.

Pest Control
The Gallery of Vegetables, which starts on page 21, points out the most notorious pests of each vegetable. For more information about your problem, see *The Ortho Problem Solver.* This reference guide includes pictures of many vegetable problems and specific information on how to control the pest.

Insects
Vigilance is the best way to control insect pests. Watch for signs of insect problems and nip them in the bud as soon as they appear. A few aphids are much easier to deal with than thousands of them. ❶ Start with the least-toxic pest control strategy, such as row covers or barriers, to exclude pests from crops altogether. ❷ When pest populations are low, handpick insects and drop them into soapy

< 18 >

water to kill them. Reach for pesticides when the pest is clearly out of control and an important crop is at risk. Be sure to select a pesticide that will control the specific pest infesting your crop.

Diseases

Sometimes correcting environmental conditions can control vegetable diseases without the need for fungicides. For example, you can prevent the spread of fungal diseases by watering with a drip hose to avoid getting foliage wet. Rotating crops, such as planting tomatoes in a new spot every year, will prevent soilborne diseases.

Weeds

❸ Like insects, weeds are best controlled with vigilance. Create conditions that favor the vegetables and suppress the weeds, then be on the lookout for interlopers and get rid of them before they set seed.

< 19 >

As crop production wanes in early fall, it's time to clean up the garden and prepare it for winter. A debris-free garden will be quick and easy to prepare for planting in spring and it will be less likely to harbor pests and diseases from the previous season. Prepare your planting plot for winter with these tips.

❶ As warm-season crops stop producing, consider replacing them with cool-season crops such as arugula, chard, kale, lettuce, radish, and spinach. The cool-season crops germinate quickly in warm soil temperatures, thrive in the cool air temperatures, and can even handle light frost.

❷ When plants die, remove them from the garden. Dead plants provide a home where pests and diseases overwinter. Pull plants up by the roots and throw them into the compost heap. If plants were diseased or plagued by insects, throw them into the trash to avoid spreading problems.

❸ In late fall, turn under any old mulch and dig out weeds. If soil is dry enough for tilling, incorporate a 3- to 4-inch layer of decomposed organic matter, such as compost, into the soil.

< 20 >

FLOWER BUD

ARTICHOKES IN ORNAMENTAL GARDEN

FLOWERS

PLANTING GUIDE	
PLANT TYPE:	Perennial
START FROM:	Seed, transplants, or divisions from an established plant
DEPTH:	Seeds: 1"; transplants: at the soil surface; divisions: 4"
SPACING:	3–6'
ROW SPACING:	6–8'
DAYS TO HARVEST:	90–100
FEATURES:	Edible flower buds

ARTICHOKES are thistles without the sting. Both the tender hearts of their large flower buds and the bases of their thick scales are edible. Where winters are mild and summers cool and foggy, artichokes are short-lived perennials that bear well for five or six years. In northern areas, grow them as annuals.

Artichokes' bold texture makes them an excellent ornamental plant. Grow them at the back of the garden for an attractive backdrop or use them as an edging plant and enjoy their texture up close. Artichokes left on the plant will open into big violet flowers.

< 22 >

Recommended cultivars

'GREEN GLOBE IMPROVED' grows best from crown divisions and is an excellent perennial cultivar. 'IMPERIAL STAR', a superb producer with a mild flavor, can be grown from seed and is both heat and cold tolerant.

How to grow

PLANTING: Start artichokes indoors six weeks before the last spring frost, sowing three seeds per 4-inch pot. Keep soil moist and warm until sprouts appear, then move the seedlings to a spot with strong light. Two weeks after germination, thin to one seedling per pot. In northern areas, encourage plants to set fruit early by moving transplants outdoors so they receive 10 to 12 days of temperatures between 32°F and 50°F; protect plants if temperatures fall below 32°F. After all danger of frost has passed, transplant seedlings into the garden.

CARE: Keep soil constantly moist for two weeks or until plants are established. Feed with water-soluble plant food just before planting and again six to eight weeks later. Mulch heavily with compost in summer to maintain soil moisture. In Zones 7 and 8 cover plants with straw over winter. Plants become less productive after the fifth or sixth year; replace with new plants grown from suckers.

PESTS: If you buy transplants, take care to purchase clean stock to avoid transmission of crown and bud decay diseases. Choose cultivars developed for resistance to curly dwarf virus and botrytis, the most common artichoke problems.

Harvest

1 Harvest artichokes before the plants bloom by cutting the flower buds when they are still immature and about 3 to 4 inches in diameter. After harvesting all buds for the season, prune the entire plant back by one-third to encourage a new crop of buds for fall harvest.

Notes

ASPARAGUS SPEARS

DORMANT CROWN

FULL GROWN ASPARAGUS IN BACK

PLANTING GUIDE	
PLANT TYPE: Perennial	
START FROM: Seed or dormant roots	
DEPTH: Seeds: ¼"; dormant roots: 6"	
SPACING: 12–24"	
ROW SPACING: 48"	
DAYS TO HARVEST: 360; spears can be harvested one year after dormant roots are planted	
FEATURES: Edible stems; long-lived perennial	

ASPARAGUS is a perennial vegetable that can flourish for 10 to 30 years. Every year each plant supplies a bountiful harvest of succulent spears for up to six weeks in spring. Once the harvest season ends, let the plants grow freely. They develop into ferny 6-foot-tall plants, which can form a backdrop for ornamentals. The stems will die back in winter, having stored up strength for the following year.

Asparagus grows best in Zones 4 to 8 and it grows year-round in California's Zone 9 where much of the commercial crop is produced.

< 24 >

Recommended cultivars

'MARY WASHINGTON' and other Washington varieties are the most popular. 'GREENWICH', 'JERSEY KNIGHT', and 'JERSEY GIANT' may have greater disease resistance and high yields.

How to grow

PLANTING: Grow asparagus from dormant crowns. Plant crowns as soon as the soil can be worked in late winter or early spring.

To plant: Dig a 6-inch-deep trench in well cultivated soil. ❶ Set the crowns in the trench, then cover them with 2 inches of soil. As the crowns sprout and rise a few inches, continue covering them with soil until the trench is filled.

CARE: Asparagus is a heavy feeder. Amend the soil annually by incorporating a 2- to 3-inch layer of well-composted horse or cow manure.

Control weeds by hand pulling or hoeing shallowly or use an herbicide labeled for the specific weed to be eradicated and for use on asparagus.

PESTS: Asparagus beetles and aphids are the most damaging pests; control them with insecticides labeled for these pests. Follow label instructions carefully so that beneficial bees are not harmed. To avoid pests, plant asparagus in an area where it has not grown for at least eight years.

Harvest

Begin harvesting when spears are at least 5 inches tall and ½ inch in diameter and have closed tips. Pick for just two weeks during the first harvest season. You can increase the harvest season to four weeks the second year and to six weeks in years thereafter.

❷ Break or cut stems off at or near ground level. Refrigerate or ice spears immediately to preserve the nutritional content and crisp texture.

After four to six weeks of harvesting, allow spears to grow into full-size plants, which produce food for next year's crop.

Notes

'KENTUCKY WONDER' POLE BEAN

LIMA BEAN

POLE BEANS

FAVA BEAN

PLANTING GUIDE	
PLANT TYPE: Annual	
START FROM: Seed	
DEPTH: 1"	
SPACING: Sow 2–3" apart; thin to 6"	
ROW SPACING: 24–36"	
DAYS TO HARVEST: 40–100	
FEATURES: Edible seeds and immature pods; easy-to-grow crop	

BEANS are a favorite vegetable of new and experienced gardeners alike. All beans need full sun and well-drained soil and, except for favas, are warm-weather crops, easily damaged by frost. They are a diverse crop. Some varieties boast colorful flowers and fruit, while others scramble up trellises; they are as pretty as they are productive. Some varieties bear both edible pods and seeds and others just edible seeds.

Bush beans, the most popular for home gardens, are excellent producers. Once the plants start producing, you'll get several quick crops in two or three weeks.

< 26 >

Recommended species and cultivars

BUSH BEANS are the most common bean in home gardens. They grow knee-high and produce edible pods about 60 days after sowing. Sow seeds after the last frost and make several small sowings three weeks apart for a long harvest. There are several types of bush beans.

SNAP BEANS have round or flat pods that vary in color from green to yellow to purple. They are your standard green bean. Harvest snap beans when the pods begin to fill out. **'VENTURE'**, **'DERBY'**, and **'PROVIDER'** are among the many dependable varieties of snap beans.

SHELL BEANS can be eaten as green snap beans; harvest when pods are young and tender. Or you can let the beans ripen until the seeds become plump and the pods feel leathery. Harvest the beans before they actually dry. Shell the beans before cooking and eating. **LIMA BEANS** fall into this category. They tolerate heat, humidity, and insects and diseases. Harvest limas when the pods are plump but still glossy. Limas can be eaten fresh, frozen, or preserved as dry beans. Fast-maturing limas, such as **'FORDHOOK 242'**, will grow in northern gardens, but other lima cultivars are most productive in areas with long summers.

DRY SHELL BEANS are similar to shell beans but are usually eaten dried. Red kidney, pinto, and black beans are examples. Allow dry beans to ripen on the plants until the pods turn brown and the plants begin to die. To harvest, pull up the plants

POLE BEANS are similar to bush beans, with one exception. They climb. Pods come in many shapes and colors. As with bush beans, there are snap, shell, and dry beans. To keep plants productive for a long time, promptly pick young pods before they develop large seeds. For pole beans with deep green pods and a long harvest, consider **'KENTUCKY BLUE'**, **'KENTUCKY WONDER'**, and **'ROMANO'**.

FAVA BEANS require cool weather and can survive temperatures as low as 10°F to 20°F. Plants are large and upright, growing to 5 feet tall. Plant fava beans in fall in climates with mild winters or in spring where summers are cool. Protein-rich fava beans are best harvested while pods are still green. Dry them for a week in a hot place, then crack open the pods. **'BROAD WINDSOR'** has excellent flavor.

Notes

_____

_____

_____

_____

more about beans > >

< 27 >

BUSH BEANS

How to grow

PLANTING: ❶ Direct-sow seeds after all danger of spring frost has passed. In areas with very short growing seasons, give beans an early start by starting seeds indoors several weeks before the last frost date. To save space, you can interplant beans with corn, sweet potatoes, and tomatoes. ❷ When plants are a few inches tall, thin them to 6 inches apart.

To create a tripod for supporting pole beans, you'll need three 6- to 8-foot-long poles. Firmly anchor the poles in the ground, tie their tops together, then sow four to six seeds at the base of each pole.

< 28 >

CARE: Beans do best when daytime temperatures are 70°F to 80°F. When temperatures rise above 85°F flowers may drop; plants are also sensitive to frost.

To encourage branching, which increases yield, cut off the tip of each pole bean vine when it gets to the top of the tripod. To hold bush plants off the soil, set stakes at the ends of each row on both sides. Tie string to the stakes 5 inches above the ground.

Bean plants are tender and easily damaged by garden tools, so weed around them by hand. Keep the soil consistently moist; water only in the morning so the plants dry quickly, which reduces the potential for disease.

Beans supply their own nitrogen but benefit from a monthly application of soluble plant food high in phosphorus and potassium.

PESTS: Beans are susceptible to several bacterial and viral diseases. Choose resistant cultivars. Fungal diseases, such as blight, rot, rust, and anthracnose, can also be a problem. Do not plant beans in the same soil year after year; instead, rotate the planting area with other vegetable crops.

The Mexican bean beetle is the main insect pest in home gardens; it lays its eggs on the undersides of bean leaves. Handpick and destroy eggs and larvae, or use neem oil for heavy infestations.

Avoid using insecticides on beans. Bean flowers attract beneficial ladybugs and predatory wasps and are pollinated by bumblebees.

Harvest

❸ Harvest by pinching or cutting pods off the plant. See page 27 for specifics for each type of bean.

Notes

_____

_____

_____

_____

'BULL'S BLOOD'

'GOLDEN'

BEETS 'CHIOGGIA'

PLANTING GUIDE	
PLANT TYPE: Annual	
START FROM: Seed	
DEPTH: ¼"	
SPACING: Sow 2" apart; thin to 4–6"	
ROW SPACING: 2–3'	
DAYS TO HARVEST: 45–60	
FEATURES: Edible roots and leaves; fast-growing, cool-weather crop	

BEETS are prized for both their sweet roots and earthy-tasting greens. A cool-season crop, beets grow best in spring and fall. Maximum color and flavor occurs when they mature in cool soil. Like all root crops, beets thrive in light-textured soil that is free of stones that may impede root growth. If you have clay or rocky soil, grow beets in raised beds.

Many varieties of this crop have bright red leaf veins. Roots may be red, yellow, white, or striped. Leaves—beet greens—and roots are edible.

< 30 >

Recommended cultivars

'RED ACE' is highly adaptable to a variety of soil and weather conditions. 'CHIOGGIA' is a very sweet striped beet. 'GOLDEN' has yellow flesh. 'BULL'S BLOOD' has stunning, sweet, dark red greens and red roots.

How to grow

PLANTING: Beets grow best in fertile, loose soil. Before planting, enrich the soil with well-decomposed compost. Sow seeds in shallow trenches filled with a mixture of compost and perlite. In areas where summers are cool, begin planting beets two to three weeks before your last spring frost. Make additional sowings of beets at three-week intervals for harvest all summer. In hot-summer climates, make a first small planting in early spring and plant again in late summer and fall.

CARE: ❶ Thin beets to 4 inches apart for best root development; eat the thinnings as greens. Mulch plants to keep roots cool and moist, and weed around them carefully by hand. If hot weather arrives before beets begin to swell, keep the roots cool by adding more mulch or hilling up loose soil around the plants.

PESTS: Aphids and flea beetles damage beets. Use floating row covers to protect seedlings from egg-laying adults.

Harvest

Beet greens can be harvested anytime, but leaves less than 4 inches tall have the most flavor. ❷ Dig or pull small globe varieties when the roots are 1 inch in diameter; dig large types when roots reach 2 inches. Leave fall crops in the ground until needed or until the soil begins to freeze. ❸ Leave an inch of foliage on roots to prevent bleeding of the strong colors, which can permanently stain porous cookware.

Notes

PLANTING GUIDE	
PLANT TYPE: Annual	
START FROM: Seed or transplants	
DEPTH: ¼–½"	
SPACING: 12–20"	
ROW SPACING: 36"	
DAYS TO HARVEST: 40–120	
FEATURES: Edible heads; good cool-weather crop	

BROCCOLI thrives in temperatures between 65°F and 80°F. It produces nutrient-rich heads when planted in early spring or late summer. If the central head is harvested before it reaches full size and before the buds open, side shoots may develop, providing harvests for an additional month if the weather remains cool.

Broccoli and other members of the cole group—cabbage, Brussels sprouts, and cauliflower—are heavy feeders. Apply a balanced water-soluble plant food every two weeks.

< 32 >

Recommended cultivars

'GREEN COMET' and 'SPARTAN EARLY' have dark green heads 7 inches across. 'GYPSY' and 'ARCADIA' mature early and are disease resistant. 'PURPLE SPROUTING' is a late fall type with small purple heads.

How to grow

PLANTING: For spring crops, start seeds indoors six weeks before your area's average last frost date. When seedlings are four weeks old, work a 3- to 4-inch layer of compost into the soil, then transplant seedlings into the garden. Protect the seedlings from cold for two to three weeks after planting, covering them with a cloche (hot cap) or cold frame.

Broccoli can also be grown as a fall crop. Start seeds indoors 10 to 12 weeks before the first fall frost. Set seedlings out when they are a month old. Or, directly sow seeds in the garden 10 to 12 weeks before the first frost date.

CARE: Water plants regularly to promote good growth. Feed with a balanced water-soluble plant food twice a month until harvest. Mulch to conserve moisture and discourage weeds. Weed carefully to avoid damaging the roots.

PESTS: Knock off aphids with a strong stream of water from the garden hose. Remove cabbage worms and loopers by hand. For serious infestations, treat plants with Ortho Bug-B-Gon Garden & Landscape Insect Killer. Discourage cabbage maggots by placing row covers over plants as soon as they are planted. Encircle seedling stems with a paper collar to discourage cutworms.

Harvest

❶ Cut heads with a sharp knife when they are tight and firm, about 55 to 85 days after seeding. When yellow flowers begin to appear, the broccoli is past its peak, although it is still edible. Side shoots often form below the cut, extending the harvest. Discard any outer leaves and inspect heads for insects before storing.

Notes

_____

_____

_____

_____

< 33 >

PLANTING GUIDE	
PLANT TYPE: Annual	
START FROM: Seed or transplants	
DEPTH: ¼–½"	
SPACING: 18–24"	
ROW SPACING: 24–42"	
DAYS TO HARVEST: 80–130	
FEATURES: Edible heads; plant in summer for harvest in fall	

BRUSSELS SPROUTS are planted in summer for harvest after frost in fall. Cool weather and frost bring out the sprouts' flavor. Brussels sprouts are a good crop for small gardens, especially when interplanted with lettuces or other quick-maturing crops.

Brussels sprouts resemble tiny cabbages in taste and appearance. Serve them steamed as an accompaniment to roasted or grilled meats.

< **34** >

Recommended cultivars

'LONG ISLAND IMPROVED' and 'CATSKILL' (a dwarf variety) are heat sensitive and best grown as fall crops. 'JADE CROSS' and 'OLIVER' mature in 90 days and are more heat tolerant than other types.

How to grow

PLANTING: Brussels sprouts require rich, fertile soil. Prepare the soil by mixing a 3- to 4-inch layer of compost into the planting bed. Direct-sow Brussels sprouts seeds into the garden 90 days before the average first fall frost in your area. Or set out transplants in late summer. Feed seedlings and transplants with Miracle-Gro Liquid Quick Start plant food and shade them from direct sun until plants become established.

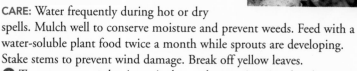

CARE: Water frequently during hot or dry spells. Mulch well to conserve moisture and prevent weeds. Feed with a water-soluble plant food twice a month while sprouts are developing. Stake stems to prevent wind damage. Break off yellow leaves.
❶ To encourage production, pinch out the growing tip when bottom sprouts are ½ inch wide.

PESTS: Knock off aphids with a strong stream of water from the garden hose. Remove cabbage worms and loopers by hand. For serious infestations, treat plants with Ortho Bug-B-Gon Garden & Landscape Insect Killer. Discourage cabbage maggots by placing row covers over plants as soon as they are planted. Encircle seedling stems with a paper collar to discourage cutworms.

Harvest

❷ Begin harvesting sprouts from the bottoms of the stalks when they are ¾ to 1½ inches in diameter. The sprouts form where leaves join the stalk, and each plant may bear 50 to 100 sprouts.

Notes

< 35 >

BALLHEAD CABBAGE

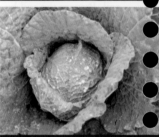

SAVOY CABBAGE

CABBAGE | **RED CABBAGE**

PLANTING GUIDE	
PLANT TYPE: Annual	
START FROM: Seed or transplants	
DEPTH: ¼–½"	
SPACING: 10–24"	
ROW SPACING: 24–42"	
DAYS TO HARVEST: 65–100	
FEATURES: Edible leaves	

CABBAGE, like broccoli, Brussels sprouts, and other cole crops, thrives in cool temperatures. In cooler climates, cabbage planted in spring will produce huge heads by late fall. In regions with hot summers it's better to plant a fast-maturing spring crop and a long-growing midseason crop for fall harvest.

Cabbages can be divided into various groups, either according to the season in which they mature (spring, summer, fall, winter) or type (savoy, looseleaf, ballhead, red, and white). Be sure to select a variety that is adapted to your climate.

< 36 >

Recommended cultivars

Early maturing types are ready for harvest in early summer and include 'FARAO' (green), 'RED EXPRESS', and 'GONZALES' (a green, dwarf variety good for small gardens). Midseason, which are harvested in summer, include 'TENDERSWEET' (green) and 'REGAL RED'. Savoy, or curly leaved, 'DRUMHEAD' and 'RED PERFECTION' require a long growing season and are harvested in fall.

How to grow

PLANTING: Start seeds indoors five to seven weeks before the last frost. ❶ Set out four- to six-week-old seedlings in soil enriched with a 2- to 3-inch layer of compost. Or set out nursery-grown transplants two weeks before the last average frost date.

CARE: ❷ Maintain consistent soil moisture to keep heads from cracking. Once seedlings are established, water with a soaker hose to avoid wetting the foliage. Weed carefully to avoid damaging the roots. Feed with a water-soluble plant food twice a month until harvest.

PESTS: Knock off aphids with a strong stream of water from the garden hose. Remove cabbage worms and loopers by hand. For serious infestations, treat plants with Ortho Bug-B-Gon Garden & Landscape Insect Killer. Discourage cabbage maggots by placing row covers over plants as soon as they are planted. Encircle seedling stems with a paper collar to discourage cutworms.

Harvest

❸ Cabbage is ready to harvest when heads are tight, firm, and 4 to 10 inches in diameter. With a sharp knife, cut the stem just below the head. Flavor is best right after harvest, but cabbage stores well for several months in cool, humid conditions.

Notes

MINI CARROTS

'CHANTENAY'

'SWEETNESS'

CARROTS

PLANTING GUIDE	
PLANT TYPE: Annual	
START FROM: Seed	
DEPTH: ¼–½"	
SPACING: Sow 1" apart; thin to 3–4"	
ROW SPACING: 12–15"	
DAYS TO HARVEST: 50–100	
FEATURES: Edible taproots and leaves; many cultivars available	

CARROTS harvested from the home garden are remarkably crisp and juicy and much more flavorful than their store-bought counterparts. Carrots grow in a wide variety of colors, shapes, and sizes. Miniature carrots that form either round roots or short blunt, cylindrical roots are good for clay soils or containers. Traditional carrots, with their large taproots, grow best in finely textured soil.

Interplant carrots among lettuces, beans, peas, tomatoes, and peppers. They grow well in raised beds. Carrots grow best in cool weather. In many areas, crops sown in the fall can be harvested through winter.

< 38 >

Recommended cultivars

'KINKO' is a 4-inch mini carrot ready to harvest in 50 to 55 days. 'ROUND ROMEO' is a smooth-skinned mini about 1 to 1½ inches in diameter. Short, early carrots ready in 65 to 70 days include 'DANVERS HALF LONG', 'SCARLET NANTES', and 'CHANTENAY'. Large carrots that are good fresh or stored, 'TENDERSWEET', 'SUGARSNAX', 'SWEETNESS', and 'BOLERO', are ready to harvest in 70 to 80 days.

How to grow

PLANTING: Carrots grow best in loose, sandy loam. Direct-sow seed two to four weeks before the last spring frost date. Moisten the soil beforehand so that the tiny seeds don't blow away. Cover seeds with ¼ inch of fine soil and water gently to avoid disturbing the seeds. In areas with long, mild autumns, you can plant a second crop in late summer.

CARE: Keep seeds evenly moist to ensure germination, which can take up to three weeks. ❶ Thin seedlings to about 3 inches apart. Weed carefully with a hoe or pull weeds by hand. Use straw or another organic mulch between rows to retain moisture and minimize weeds, but keep it off the leafy tops.

You can harvest fall-sown carrots all winter. ❷ Cut off the green tops to about an inch and mulch plants heavily with straw. In areas with extreme winters, also place a cold frame over them.

PESTS: No significant pests in the home garden.

Harvest

Begin pulling carrots as soon as their shoulders poke out of the ground and begin to develop color. This is a good way to thin rows to give the remaining carrots a chance to grow larger. In northern zones, wait until the ground has begun to freeze before digging the rest of the carrots; cold weather increases their sweet flavor.

Notes

CAULIFLOWER

GREEN CAULIFLOWER (TOP LEFT), WHITE (BOTTOM LEFT)

'ANDES' CAULIFLOWER

'GRAFFITI'

'ALVERDA'

PLANTING GUIDE	
PLANT TYPE: Annual	
START FROM: Seed or transplants	
DEPTH: ¼–½"	
SPACING: 12–30"	
ROW SPACING: 24–36"	
DAYS TO HARVEST: 55–90	
FEATURES: Edible heads; excellent cool-season crop	

CAULIFLOWER flourishes in spring and early fall. Although it requires slightly more care than some other garden vegetables, the reward of a crunchy, flavorful crop is worth the effort. Along with the standard white cauliflower, novel purple- and green-head types are available.

Fast-maturing hybrids are best for spring or fall crops. Except in the cool temperatures of the far North, it is best to plant any variety that requires more than 80 days to mature in the fall. Purple-head types need a lot of space but are heat and cold tolerant and freeze well. All varieties are intriguing, tasty, and packed with nutrients.

< 40 >

Recommended cultivars

'EARLY SNOWBALL' matures quickly on small plants that fit well in a petite garden.
'GRAFFITI' produces bright purple heads and 'ALVERDA' has green heads.

How to grow

PLANTING: For spring harvest, sow seeds indoors four weeks before the last frost date. Transplant seedlings into the garden after the last chance of frost has passed. For fall harvest sow seeds outdoors 90 days before the first frost date.

CARE: Mulch plants and water regularly to keep soil cool and moist. Weed carefully by hand, taking care not to damage the plants. Cauliflower does not tolerate stress well and responds by blooming prematurely. The result is an undeveloped head called a button.

To ensure a bright white head, you need to cover the head while it is developing. This is called blanching. ❶ Pull the longest leaves up and over the head; be sure the head is dry. ❷ Secure the leaves in place with twine or strips of soft nylon. Begin blanching as soon as the head starts to form. Purple and green heads do not need to be blanched.

PESTS: Knock off aphids with a strong stream of water from a garden hose. Remove cabbage worms and loopers by hand. For serious infestations, treat plants with Ortho Bug-B-Gon Garden & Landscape Insect Killer. Place row covers over the plants to prevent cabbage maggots from laying eggs or feeding on the leaves. Encircle seedling stems with a paper collar to discourage cutworms.

Harvest

Cauliflower is ready to harvest when the heads are about 6 to 8 inches in diameter. When the curds begin to separate, the head is past its peak. Harvest by cutting just below the head. To store heads for two to three weeks, cut farther down so you can wrap some leaves around the heads.

Notes

_____

_____

_____

< 41 >

'RUBY'

'BRIGHT LIGHTS'

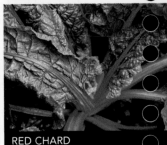

CHARD   RED CHARD

PLANTING GUIDE	
PLANT TYPE: Annual	
START FROM: Seed or transplants	
DEPTH: ⅓–½"	
SPACING: Sow 1" apart; thin to 6"	
ROW SPACING: 30–36"	
DAYS TO HARVEST: 50–55	
FEATURES: Edible leaves and stalks; colorful stalks are ornamental	

CHARD is happiest in cool weather, but it also copes with hot summers. It is related to spinach but is much slower to bolt (send up a flower stalk, which results in the leaves becoming inedible). Chard may grow in the garden all summer. Cultivars with bright-hued stems are often grown for their ornamental qualities as well as their edible leaves. Plants are moderately winter hardy.

Eat young leaves raw in salads. Cook mature leaves as you would spinach.

< 42 >

Recommended cultivars

'FORDHOOK GIANT' is a dependable, hardy dark green chard with white ribs. 'RHUBARB' has red ribs. 'BRIGHT LIGHTS' and 'RAINBOW' ribs offer a mix of vivid reds and yellows.

How to grow

PLANTING: Sow seeds directly in the garden two to three weeks before the last frost. Soak seeds overnight before planting them. Keep the soil constantly moist until seedlings are established, then mulch with straw to keep roots cool and moist.

CARE: Thin young plants to 2 inches apart; use the thinnings in salads. Apply a balanced water-soluble plant food twice a month. Cut plants back to 3 inches in late summer to rejuvenate them for fall production.

PESTS: Several pests sometimes bother chard. If aphids and leaf miners attack the plants, remove and destroy affected leaves. Pick off corn borer larvae by hand. ❶ Young leaves may show evidence of beetle feeding; dust with rotenone. Use bait or traps for slugs and snails. Powdery mildew is the main disease affecting chard; choose resistant varieties.

Harvest

Begin harvesting chard when the leaves are about 5 inches tall. ❷ Break or cut off one or two outer leaves at a time from each plant, leaving the inner leaves to develop.

Notes

_____
_____
_____
_____
_____
_____
_____
_____
_____
_____

< **43** >

'KANDY KWIK'

'SENECA' READY
FOR HARVEST

CORN PLANTED
IN BLOCKS

MALE CORN FLOWERS OR TASSELS

PLANTING GUIDE

PLANT TYPE:	Annual
START FROM:	Seed
DEPTH:	1"
SPACING:	Sow 3" apart; thin to 9–12"
ROW SPACING:	24–36"
DAYS TO HARVEST:	60–95
FEATURES:	Edible seeds

CORN is a summer treat. It requires warm weather and more space than most vegetables, but today's hybrids can be grown close together if you fertilize them. Still, the minimum requirement for a successful planting of sweet corn is a sunny spot at least 6 feet long and 5 feet wide.

Sweet corn varies by the amount of sugar the kernels contain. Old-fashioned varieties contain less sugar than new hybrids. You will also find a range of kernel colors. Look for white, yellow, and bicolored varieties.

< **44** >

Recommended cultivars

Some varieties of corn will cross-pollinate, which can result in all the plants producing starchy kernels. To avoid this problem in a small garden, plant cultivars that do not form silks at the same time.

'SENECA' is popular in northern zones. 'KANDY' cultivars grow well in warm climates and are available in early, midseason, and late varieties. Try 'GOLDEN MIDGET' in small gardens, where its 3-foot stalks and 4-inch ears take up little room. 'FLEET' bears bicolor ears in 65 days.

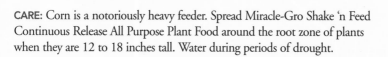

How to grow

PLANTING: Direct-sow corn about two weeks after the last frost date. Because corn is pollinated by the wind, plant the seeds in blocks of three or more in each direction instead of in rows. Planting in blocks also helps protect shallow-rooted corn from toppling over in high winds.

CARE: Corn is a notoriously heavy feeder. Spread Miracle-Gro Shake 'n Feed Continuous Release All Purpose Plant Food around the root zone of plants when they are 12 to 18 inches tall. Water during periods of drought.

PESTS: Choose cultivars that are resistant to leaf blight, smut, and bacterial wilt. Flea beetles feeding on leaves can infect plants with bacterial wilt disease; place floating row covers over young plants to prevent infection. Use seed pretreated with fungicide to control seed rot and seedling blight. ❶ Control earworm with regular applications of labeled insecticide spray. Use fencing around the garden to keep out deer and raccoons.

Harvest

Pick sweet corn ears in the milk stage—when kernels are fully formed but not mature, about 20 days after the first silks appear. Carefully peel back the husk on an ear to see if it is ready. ❷ The kernels should be plump and squirt a milky juice when punctured. Most types remain in the milk stage for less than a week, so check frequently.

Notes

'BURPLESS BUSH'

'MARKETMORE 97'

VINING CUCUMBER PLANT

'FANCIPAK' PICKLING

PLANTING GUIDE	
PLANT TYPE: Annual	
START FROM: Seed	
DEPTH: ½"	
SPACING: Sow 12" apart; thin to 24"	
ROW SPACING: 5–6'	
DAYS TO HARVEST: 50–70	
FEATURES: Edible fruit; vigorous grower and producer	

CUCUMBERS are easy to grow and often produce more fruit than most gardeners can use. Limit the size of plantings unless you plan to make lots of pickles. Six plants of any type provide plenty of fruit to eat and share. Cucumbers are available in bush or vining types. Bush cukes are compact plants, ideal for containers. Vining types will crawl across the ground or with training will climb a trellis.

For pickling, grow small-fruited pickling cucumbers that produce dozens of small fruit all at once. Slicing cukes have straight fruit. Burpless varieties have thin, tender skin, which makes them easy to digest.

< **46** >

Recommended cultivars

PICKLING: 'LITTLE LEAF' sets fruit without pollination and yields well even during dry spells. 'NORTHERN PICKLING' produces fruit in 45 to 50 days. 'FANCIPAK' is a disease-resistant heirloom variety.

SLICING: 'MARKETMORE' and 'GENERAL LEE' cultivars are popular types. 'DIVA' is an award-winning seedless type that cucumber beetles don't seem to like.

How to grow

PLANTING: Before planting, incorporate generous amounts of compost or other organic matter into the soil. ❶ Direct-sow seed when soil and air temperatures reach at least 60°F. Plant cucumbers in rows or hills of five to seven seeds. Or plant nursery-grown transplants after the last average frost date.

CARE: Thin to three plants per hill or to 6 to 9 inches apart in rows. Keep the soil continuously moist, giving plants at least ½ inch of water per week. Increase watering during periods of high heat. Use row covers to protect young plants from pests and cold. Even a light frost will kill cucumbers. For vining types, install trellises or other supports.

PESTS: Cucumbers are susceptible to many problems. ❷ Cucumber beetles are the most significant pests; they spread bacterial wilt. Pick off and destroy any you find. New hybrids have been developed for disease resistance. Choose cultivars that have been bred specifically for your climate. Use insecticides and fungicides when problems get out of hand. Follow label directions and pay particular attention to timing to avoid killing pollinators.

Harvest

Harvest slicing varieties when they are 8 to 12 inches long and pickling types when 2 inches or longer. Picking frequently increases production; pick daily to prevent fruits from becoming too large.

Notes

_____

_____

_____

< 47 >

'NEON'

'EASTER EGG'

EGGPLANT   'ROSA BIANCA'

PLANTING GUIDE	
PLANT TYPE: Annual	
START FROM: Transplants; can be direct-sown in southern zones	
DEPTH: ¼–½"	
SPACING: 18–24"	
ROW SPACING: 24–48"	
DAYS TO HARVEST: 60–90	
FEATURES: Edible fruit; thrives in hot, humid conditions	

EGGPLANTS are available in a range of sizes and shapes. The most popular cultivars for the home garden are small types, which mature sooner than the ones commonly found at grocery stores. There are very long, thin eggplants, as well as finger-size, egg-size, and walnut-size cultivars. Eggplants' silky skin ranges from lavender to black to white.

Eggplant revels in high heat and humidity. Where nights are consistently cooler than 65°F, the plants may fail to set fruit altogether. A perennial in tropical climates, eggplant grows as an annual in the vegetable garden.

< 48 >

Recommended cultivars

'ICHIBAN' bears elongated purple fruits in 65 days. 'NEON' bears medium-size bright pinkish-purple fruits. 'BLACK' is a dark purple cultivar with 4- to 6-inch fruits ready in 70 to 75 days. 'ROSA BIANCA' is an Italian eggplant with almost round, white blushed with purple fruit. 'BLACK BEAUTY' is an heirloom variety with plump, large fruits ready for harvest in 80 to 85 days. 'EASTER EGG' has white fruit.

How to grow

PLANTING: Direct-sow eggplant seed in hot climates. In northern areas buy or start your own transplants. Sow seeds indoors eight weeks before the last frost date. Hold off on setting plants in the garden until at least two weeks after the last frost.

CARE: To produce reliably, most eggplant varieties require 60 days of night temperatures 70°F to 80°F. In cool climates with short seasons you often can boost yield by growing eggplant under tunnels or row covers. Eggplant is a heavy feeder. Enrich soil with a 2-inch layer of compost around plants. Feed once a month with water-soluble plant food.

PESTS: Watch for Colorado potato beetles and flea beetles. ❶ Flea beetles, a common pest, riddle the leaves with holes; use row covers to protect plants. Shake or knock Colorado potato beetles off plants and onto a sheet early in the morning, then destroy them.

Harvest

❷ Harvest fruits when they reach full cultivar color and are firm and glossy. ❸ Cut off ripe fruits. Harvest regularly to promote continued fruiting.

Notes

_____

_____

_____

< 49 >

PLANTING GUIDE	
PLANT TYPE: Annual	
START FROM: Seed or transplants	
DEPTH: ¼–½"	
SPACING: 5–7"	
ROW SPACING: 12–18"	
DAYS TO HARVEST: 75–100	
FEATURES: Edible leaves and bulbs	

FENNEL is a cool-season, Italian vegetable also known as finocchio or Florence fennel. The leaves have the classic fragrance and flavor of the herb fennel, but this vegetable's main attraction is its crisp aboveground bulbs. Made up of flattened stalks similar to those of celery, the bulb has a nutty, slightly aniselike flavor, which becomes sweeter when cooked.

Common fennel, the perennial herb, is closely related. It does not form a swollen base and is grown instead for its feathery, anise-flavored foliage and seeds.

< 50 >

Recommended cultivars

'ZEFA FINO' has a large bulb and is slow to bolt. In northern zones, try fast-maturing 'ORION', which is ready to harvest in 75 to 80 days. 'HERALD' is good for early planting and resists bolting.

How to grow

PLANTING: Fennel seedlings exposed to cold weather, which can happen when you plant in the spring, tend to bolt—go to seed—prematurely and fail to form the bulb. While you can plant fennel in spring, it is better to sow it in summer for harvest in mid- to late fall. In much of the southern United States, August is the best month for planting.

Seeds germinate well in hot soil if you keep the soil consistently moist. You can also start plants indoors, setting them out when they develop a tuft of ferny leaves.

CARE: Water during dry periods to help prevent bolting. Fennel is a heavy feeder. Apply a water-soluble plant food every two weeks. ❶ If plants have a tendency to flop, hold them upright by tying their stems to a bamboo stake with twine.

When bulbs reach about 2 inches in diameter, blanch them by mounding soil or mulch around the entire plant, leaving just the feathery top uncovered.

PESTS: No significant problems affect fennel.

Harvest

Harvest fennel when the bulbs are about 3 inches in diameter, about 80 to 100 days after planting. ❷ Harvest by digging the entire plant. Cut off the roots and the tops of the longest leaves. Remove the outermost two or three stems from the bulb. These tend to be tough and stringy.

Notes

_____
_____
_____
_____
_____

< 51 >

HARDNECK GARLIC

SOFTNECK GARLIC

ELEPHANT AND
RED GARLIC

PLANTING GUIDE

PLANT TYPE: Herbaceous perennial usually grown as an annual

START FROM: Cloves split from a bulb

DEPTH: 2"

SPACING: 6"

ROW SPACING: 12–15"

DAYS TO HARVEST: 90–110 days

FEATURES: Edible bulb

GARLIC is easy to grow and very productive. Fall is the best time to plant garlic, with the exception of elephant garlic, which should be planted first thing in spring.

There are three types of garlic: softneck, hardneck, and elephant. Softneck is similar to the garlic sold in grocery stores. It is composed of several large cloves on the outside and many small cloves inside. Softneck garlic keeps well and has a strong flavor. Hardneck garlic is the most cold hardy. It is milder and the cloves are easier to peel than those of softneck. Elephant garlic produces huge cloves with a mild flavor. It is the least cold hardy; plant it in spring.

< 52 >

Recommended cultivars

'GERMAN PORCELAIN' is a popular hardneck garlic with white-skinned cloves. 'KILLARNEY RED' is a hardneck with large pink-skinned cloves. Good softnecks include 'SILVERSKIN' and 'CALIFORNIA EARLY'.

How to grow

PLANTING: ❶ Break bulbs apart into individual cloves, leaving the skin intact. ❷ Plant the cloves pointed end up in well-drained, fertile loam. Plant garlic in midautumn or early spring in northern areas and in late autumn or early winter in the South.

CARE: Garlic needs regular moisture, but it will rot in soil that is wet all the time. Apply water-soluble plant food, such as Miracle-Gro Water Soluble All Purpose, once a week until the foliage starts to brown before harvest. Keep beds weeded and cut off flowers to encourage bulb production. ❸ If growing garlic over winter, spread a layer of straw mulch over the soil.

PESTS: Soilborne diseases and insects may be problematic; avoid them by planting garlic in a different spot each year. Pink rot and mildew can be problems in warm, humid climates; allow for ample air circulation and discard infected plants.

Harvest

Push over plant tops and stop watering when about half the lower leaves begin to turn brown. Let bulbs cure for a week in the garden like this, then dig them and hang them for a week in a dry, shady location with good air circulation. Trim off stalks and cut roots close to the base of each bulb. Store the bulbs in mesh bags in a cool (35°F to 55°F), dry location. Save the largest cloves for planting next season.

Notes

_____

_____

_____

LEEK

PLANTING GUIDE

PLANT TYPE:	Annual
START FROM:	Seeds or transplants
DEPTH:	¼–½"
SPACING:	4–6"
ROW SPACING:	24–30"
DAYS TO HARVEST:	70–150 days
FEATURES:	Edible stems; frost tolerant

LEEKS have thick stems of tightly wrapped leaves. This cold-hardy crop is easy to grow for fall, winter, or spring harvest. Leeks thrive in well-drained soil that is rich in organic matter. In gardens with clay soil, plant bulbs in a raised bed amended with compost.

The lower portions of the leaves are edible and have an onion flavor that is delicious in soups and potato dishes.

< 54 >

Recommended cultivars

'OTINA' has long blue-green leaves; it is frost-tender. 'VARNA' is a fast-growing cultivar with slender, self-blanching stalks. 'JOLANT', a miniature variety, has a mild flavor and is a good choice for small gardens. 'RIKOR' is early, vigorous, tall, and sweet. Long-season, winter-hardy 'GIANT MUSSELBURGH' has juicy, thick stalks; it is cold tolerant and good for both northern and southern gardens.

How to grow

PLANTING: Sow seeds indoors eight weeks before the average last frost date. ❶ Move seedlings to the garden around the last frost date. Or direct-sow leeks four weeks before the last frost. Leeks can also be started from transplants purchased at a nursery.

CARE: Feed fast-growing leeks with a water-soluble plant food, such as Miracle-Gro Water Soluble All Purpose, twice a month. Water as needed to keep soil moist but not waterlogged.
❷ To increase the amount of white shank on the stalk, blanch the stems by mounding soil around them, or plant the leeks in the bottom of trenches, gradually filling in with soil as the stems grow.

PESTS: No significant pests affect leeks.

Harvest

❸ Harvest leeks when the stem base is about an inch in diameter. ❹ In cool regions, dig plants and store in a cool location before the first frost date, or leave them in the garden under heavy mulch and harvest as needed. Dig any remaining leeks in spring.

Notes

LETTUCE

BUTTERHEAD-TYPE LEAF LETTUCE

BIBB LEAF LETTUCE

ROMAINE LETTUCE

RED LOOSELEAF LETTUCE

PLANTING GUIDE

PLANT TYPE: Annual

START FROM: Seed or transplants

DEPTH: ¼–½"

SPACING: Sow 1" apart; thin to 8–10" apart

ROW SPACING: 12–24"

DAYS TO HARVEST: 45–85

FEATURES: Edible leaves; excellent cool-season crop

LETTUCE is a palate-pleasing cool-season crop. One of the great joys of growing lettuce is experimenting with the many varieties available. Leaf lettuce forms a loose head and varies in size, color, and texture. Butterhead types have a delicate flavor and are easy to grow. Crisphead lettuce, such as iceberg, needs a long growing period in cool weather. It is the most challenging type to grow at home. Looseleaf lettuce includes varieties with red and crinkly leaves as well as those with traditional green leaves. Romaine types are sturdy, upright plants that have the best flavor when they mature in cool weather.

< 56 >

Recommended cultivars

HEAD LETTUCE: 'ITHACA' is heat tolerant and slow to bolt. 'SIERRA' grows best in cool coastal areas.

LEAF LETTUCE: 'BUTTERCRUNCH' and 'SUMMER BIBB' are heat tolerant. 'BOSTON' and 'FOUR SEASONS' mature early.

LOOSELEAF LETTUCE: 'SALAD BOWL', 'OAKLEAF', and 'RED DEER TONGUE' are heat tolerant but do best in shade. 'RED SAILS' has crinkly leaves with burgundy edges.

ROMAINE: At 5 to 7 inches, 'LITTLE GEM' is good for small gardens.

How to grow

PLANTING: ❶ Start head lettuce indoors six weeks before the last frost date; transplant outside in three weeks. Direct-sow other lettuces in early spring or fall. Successive plantings ensure prolonged harvest. Seedlings will tolerate light frost.

CARE: Thin seedlings as needed. Pull weeds by hand or hoe lightly to avoid disturbing the shallow roots. Keep soil consistently moist but not waterlogged, and mulch to hold in moisture and cool soil.

PESTS: Purchase seed that has been pretreated with fungicide to prevent damping off and downy mildew. Thin plants to the correct spacing to avoid fungal diseases. Handpick beetles and caterpillars; use row covers as pest barriers. Knock off aphids with a strong stream of water.

Harvest

Leaf lettuce is the fastest-growing type and can be picked when leaves are as small as 2 inches. ❷ Cut or pinch off outer leaves; new leaves will continue to form. Pull up plants when they are 4 to 6 inches tall, before plants bolt, or go to seed; leaves turn tough and bitter in heat and then plants bolt. Harvest individual outer leaves of butterhead and romaine lettuce or cut off the entire head about an inch above the soil surface; a new head may grow. Pick head lettuce when the center is firm.

Notes

MELONS

MELONS REQUIRE LOTS OF ROOM

'CHARENTAIS' CANTALOUPE

MUSKMELON

'EARLY CRISP' HONEY DEW

PLANTING GUIDE	
PLANT TYPE: Annual	
START FROM: Seed or transplants	
DEPTH: ½"	
SPACING: 2–8'	
ROW SPACING: 5–7'	
DAYS TO HARVEST: 70–100	
FEATURES: Edible fruit; warm-season vining plant	

MELONS are easy to grow in the home garden and often produce several fruits per vine. Space is a consideration when growing melons. Their sprawling vines need about 10 square feet of growing space.

Three types of melons are well-suited to the home garden: true cantaloupes, muskmelons, and winter melons. True cantaloupes have a warty, ribbed rind and sweet, bright-orange flesh. Muskmelons have netted, yellowish rinds and orange flesh. Winter melons vary in appearance. For example, honeydews have a smooth rind and green flesh; crenshaws have yellow rind and salmon-pink flesh.

< 58 >

Recommended cultivars

CANTALOUPE: 'CHARENTAIS' is an early, small melon.

MUSKMELON: 'AMBROSIA' has a small seed cavity and sweet flesh.

WINTER MELON: 'BURPEE'S EARLY HYBRID' is a large yellow-green crenshaw with pink flesh. 'HONEY PEAR' is a medium-size pale gold honeydew that has almost white flesh.

How to grow

PLANTING: Start seeds indoors in peat pots one month before the last frost. One to two weeks after the last frost, move seedlings or purchased transplants to the garden. Or direct-sow five to seven seeds in hills. Thin to two or three seedlings per hill.

CARE: Water consistently, especially while plants are flowering and fruits developing. In dry climates or during periods of drought, provide at least 1 inch of water weekly. Plants need less water when fruit is ripening. Feed at planting, again when fruits begin to form, and about two weeks after fruit-set. Use a low-nitrogen, high-phosphorus, high-potassium plant food.

Protect ripening melons by setting them on inverted pots, boards, or pieces of cardboard. Melons grow best when air temperatures average 70°F. Cool or cloudy weather and too much moisture during fruit development lessen flavor. Provide early-season warmth with plastic tunnels.

PESTS: Striped and spotted cucumber beetles are the worst pests, spreading bacterial wilt; handpick and destroy. Aphids can be troublesome; knock them off with a blast of water. Choose varieties resistant to fusarium wilt, anthracnose, black rot, powdery mildew, and other diseases.

Harvest

Melons ripen from mid- to late summer or early autumn. ❶ Usually, fruit is ripe when the stem easily separates from the fruit. Other clues include deeply colored rind and yellowing or softening at the blossom end of the fruit.

Notes

< 59 >

'BURGUNDY' OKRA

HARVESTING OKRA

PLANTING GUIDE	
PLANT TYPE: Annual	
START FROM: Seed or transplants	
DEPTH: ¼"	
SPACING: 12"	
ROW SPACING: 24–36"	
DAYS TO HARVEST: 40–80	
FEATURES: Edible pods	

OKRA thrives in long, hot summers. In cool climates, it grows less vigorously but will produce, just not as much as in warm regions. Where it does thrive, a single spring sowing will yield nonstop tender fruits until frost.

The plant's flowers are lovely, like hollyhocks, but the large, coarse nature of the plant disqualifies it as a favorite edible ornamental. Okra tolerates dry soil; avoid planting in rich soil, which will cause it to produce large leaves and few fruits.

< 60 >

Recommended cultivars

'CLEMSON SPINELESS' grows well in the North as well as the South. 'RED VELVET' has wine-red pods and stems. Early-yielding 'CAJUN DELIGHT' is good in northern gardens. Dwarf 'BABY BUBBA' works well in containers and small spaces. 'BURGUNDY' has red pods.

How to grow

PLANTING: You can direct-sow okra—soak seeds overnight in warm water beforehand—or plant transplants. Wait to plant until after the danger of frost has passed and the soil temperature has been above 60°F for at least two weeks. Be sure to keep soil moist until plants are established.

CARE: Feed transplants with a starter solution, such as Miracle-Gro Liquid Quick Start to prevent transplant shock. Spray water-soluble plant food such as Miracle-Gro Water Soluble All Purpose on all plants every two to four weeks.

Prune plants in late summer to encourage growth of lateral branches, which will produce new flowers and pods. Cut the main stem back by one-third of its length, then water plants well to promote new growth.

PESTS: Okra is susceptible to root-knot nematodes and fusarium wilt, and to southern blight in hot, humid regions. Planting okra in a different spot every year is the best control.

Harvest

Pods mature 60 days after flowering. They can quickly become tough, so harvest frequently when fruit is 3 to 5 inches long. ❶ To harvest, gently pull the pods away from the stem and clip free with sharp scissors.

Cut pods release a sticky substance, which puts off many people. Cook pods whole with the caps still attached to minimize it.

Notes

_____

_____

_____

_____

_____

_____

_____

< 61 >

'MAMBO'

'EARLY YELLOW GLOBE' LONG-DAY ONION

'COPRA'

PLANTING GUIDE	
PLANT TYPE: Annual	
START FROM: Seed, transplants, or dormant bulbs called sets	
DEPTH: ½"	
SPACING: Sow seeds ½"; thin to 3–10"	
ROW SPACING: 12–18"	
DAYS TO HARVEST: 55–300	
FEATURES: Edible bulb and stem	

ONIONS are grown and harvested in many different forms. Cultivate onions for their immature green stems, called scallions; for their young bulbs, called green onions; or for their mature, storable bulbs. Shallots, onions that grow in clusters of 3 to 10 bulbs, are grown for use as dried bulbs and have a delicate flavor.

Choose onions based on their day-length requirements. Short-day varieties do best in warm climates, while long-day cultivars thrive in cool climates. Onions are heavy feeders requiring rich, well-drained soil.

< 62 >

Recommended cultivars

SHORT-DAY VARIETIES: 'YELLOW GRANEX' matures in early summer. 'RED CREOLE' has a pungent flavor. 'NEW MEXICO WHITE GRANO' is a large, mild white onion.

LONG-DAY VARIETIES: 'EARLY YELLOW GLOBE' stores well and is good fresh. 'MAMBO' stores well. 'COPRA' dries quickly for storage.

How to grow

PLANTING: Direct-sow seed in rows a month before the last average frost date. Thin the rows throughout the season, using the thinnings as scallions or green onions.

❶ Plant sets and transplants in early spring in northern areas and in fall in warmer climates. Grow them in rows with the pointed end just showing above ground.

CARE: Water as needed during dry conditions. Weed frequently to reduce competition for nutrients. Remove seed heads, if they form. Mulch to prevent sunscald on bulbs. Use water-soluble plant food twice a month during the growing season.

PESTS: Onions are susceptible to thrips, maggots, and soilborne diseases; to avoid, it's best to plant in a different area each year. Shallots are susceptible to pink rot, particularly in the South; treat soil with fungicide.

Harvest

❷ Dig or pull scallions and green shallots when the tops are 4 to 8 inches tall; green onions are ready when the tops are 6 to 8 inches tall and bulbs have begun to swell. Dig or pull up plants.

If you plan to store onions and shallots, stop watering when the green tops have withered and browned. After a week, dig up shallots; leave onions in the ground for two weeks, then dig them up. Place harvested bulbs in a dry, shady spot for one week. When completely dry, cut off stalks and roots, then hang the bulbs in mesh bags in a cool, dry location.

Notes

_____

_____

_____

< 63 >

SHELLING PEAS

'LITTLE MARVEL'

'TALL TELEPHONE'

'SUPER SUGAR SNAP'

PLANTING GUIDE	
PLANT TYPE:	Annual
START FROM:	Seed
DEPTH:	½–1"
SPACING:	3–4"
ROW SPACING:	24–48"
DAYS TO HARVEST:	55–75
FEATURES: Edible seeds; some varieties have edible pods	

PEAS are a diverse group. Choose among shelling peas—also called garden peas—and edible-pod peas (snap and snow peas). Shell peas are grown for the round seeds within the pods. Snow peas have small peas and sweet pods that stay tender when they mature. They are heavy producers. Snap peas have both full-size seeds and edible pods.

Peas thrive in cool weather. They tolerate brief periods of temperatures below 25°F, but prolonged exposure will interfere with development. Peas are vines that climb by tendrils. There are bush type plants in each group of peas.

< 64 >

Recommended cultivars
Shelling peas

'DAKOTA' is an early variety ready to harvest in 50 to 55 days. Its vines are short enough to be grown without support. 'CASELOAD' is an extra-sweet shelling pea ready in 55 to 60 days. It is slow to become starchy when harvested regularly. 'MAESTRO' and 'ECLIPSE' are good choices for hot southern areas. They are disease resistant and ready in 60 to 65 days. 'ALDERMAN', sometimes called 'TALL TELEPHONE', grows 5 feet or more tall and bears long pods, each with eight to 10 extremely sweet peas in 75 days. It requires a strong support system.

'GREEN ARROW' and 'THOMAS LAXTON' are older varieties that are famous for their rich pea flavor. 'ALASKA' is a short-season variety. It is ready in just 55 days and is good for canning. 'OREGON TRAIL' is ready in 55 to 70 days and is a prolific producer of small pods with sweet peas. It is delicious raw or cooked. 'LITTLE MARVEL' and 'WANDO' are both ready in 60 to 70 days. They tolerate heat well.

Edible-pod peas

SNOW PEAS: 'OREGON GIANT' is a disease-resistant variety that produces sweet, large pods in 60 to 70 days and throughout the summer. 'SUGAR POD 2' is a good choice for cool areas. It is ready to harvest in 60 to 70 days. 'HO LOHN DOW' has large pods and is ready in 60 to 70 days. 'SNOW GREEN' has crisp, flavorful pods.

SNAP PEAS: 'SUGAR ANN' is the earliest snap-pea variety. It is ready to harvest in 50 to 55 days. 'SUGAR SNAP' produces plump, succulent pods in 60 to 70 days in both cool and hot weather. Remove the strings on the pods before eating or cooking them. 'SNAPPY' is sweet and shows some disease resistance. 'SUGAR SPRINT' is a delicious, nearly stringless snap pea. 'SUGAR POP' and 'SUGAR DADDY' are stringless varieties. 'SUPER SUGAR SNAP' is resistant to powdery mildew.

Notes

_____
_____
_____
_____
_____
_____
_____

more about peas > >

< 65 >

BUSH PEAS

How to grow

PLANTING: ❶ Plant peas in early spring in a location where they can be protected from midday sun if temperatures are over 80°F. Grow peas in rich, moist, well-drained soil. Peas do well interplanted with corn, tomatoes, garlic, onions, and lettuce.

CARE: Keep the soil consistently moist and weed by hand to avoid disturbing tender vines and roots. Most peas have weak stems that need support. ❷ A 5-foot trellis made of fence wire, string, or polyester netting will do the job. Or you can support them with pea brush. Save twiggy branches when you prune your shrubs. Poke the cut ends into the soil down the center of the row. Bush types tend to prop up one another well.

< 66 >

PESTS: Peas are susceptible to numerous diseases including leaf spot, scab, blights, rots, fusarium wilt, powdery mildew, botrytis and other molds, damping-off, and mosaic virus. Choose cultivars bred for resistance to bacteria and fungi common in your area. Plant peas in a different area each year to avoid diseases that persist in the soil.

Harvest

❸ Shelling peas are ready to pick when the pea seeds are fully rounded. Store unshelled peas for up to three days and shelled peas for up to seven days. Leave some pods to dry on the vine if you want to keep seed for next year's crop. Pick mature peas regularly for best flavor and to promote the development of other pods.

Harvest snow peas while the pods are still flat and the seeds inside are small and undeveloped.

Pick snap and other edible-pod varieties when the pods are plump and the seeds are fully developed. Store edible-pod peas in the refrigerator for up to one week or blanch and freeze them for up to one year.

Notes

_____

_____

_____

_____

_____

_____

_____

_____

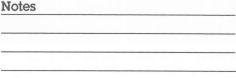

< 67 >

'MEXIBELL' SWEET BELL PEPPER

YELLOW SWEET BELL

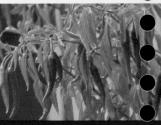

BANANA SWEET PEPPER

'THAI DRAGON' HOT PEPPER

PLANTING GUIDE	
PLANT TYPE: Annual	
START FROM: Seed or transplants	
DEPTH: ¼"	
SPACING: 12–24"	
ROW SPACING: 30–36"	
DAYS TO HARVEST: 60–90	
FEATURES: Edible fruit in a variety of colors, shapes, and flavors	

PEPPERS vary in shape, size, color, and heat. They grow best when temperatures range between 60°F and 80°F. In long summers or in the South, sweet bell peppers mature from green to yellow, orange, red, brown, purple, or black. Hot peppers develop more heat in hot climates, but they will grow well in the North.

There are three groups of peppers: sweet bell peppers, sweet nonbell peppers, and hot peppers. Sweet bells are the blocky pepper that is easily found at the grocery store. Sweet nonbells often have a tapered or irregular shape. Hot peppers have a pungent flavor.

< 68 >

Recommended cultivars
Sweet bell peppers

'CALIFORNIA WONDER' and 'WHOPPER IMPROVED' have high yields over a long period and resist viruses. 'LABRADOR' ripens to bright yellow. 'RED BEAUTY' produces fire-engine red fruits. 'BIG EARLY' produces enormous red bells up to 8 inches long and 4 inches in diameter. 'JUPITER' has large green fruits with an excellent sweet flavor.

'ACE' is prolific and resistant to blossom drop, producing small red bells. 'LIPSTICK' is an early, short, lobeless tapering bell that ripens to an extremely sweet red. 'TEQUILA' bells start out purple and fade to red as they mature; harvest the fruit at any point of maturity. 'MEXIBELL' has large fruit that is good for stuffing.

For a sweet pepper that is ornamental as well as tasty, try 'ROUMANIAN RAINBOW'. The fruits turn from ivory to orange to red; plants often have peppers in all states of coloration simultaneously.

Sweet nonbell peppers

'BANANA SUPREME' is an 8-inch early banana pepper that ripens to red. For frying peppers that are also good in salads, try 'CUBANELLE'. 'CORNO DI TORO ROSSO' produces many bull's-horn-shaped red fruits on tall sturdy plants. 'SWEET CAYENNE' and 'JIMMY NARDELLO' look like long, hot cayenne peppers but actually are among the sweetest nonbell peppers available.

For container growing, try 'SWEET PICKLE', an edible ornamental plant that holds its 2-inch yellow, orange, red, and purple peppers upright on compact plants. 'CHILLY CHILI' peppers look like little cayennes but are not hot. The compact, colorful, and extremely heat-tolerant plants are perfect for patio containers.

Hot peppers

'ROBUSTINI' is a mildly hot pepper good for salads or for pickling. 'PAPRIKA SUPREME' has tapered, sweet red fruits with just a hint of warmth. 'HUNGARIAN HOT WAX' has fruits that ripen from pale yellow to bright red and are good for frying and pickling.

Extremely hot peppers include prolific 'SUPER CHILI'; small but extremely hot 'HABANERO'; and high-yielding 'THAI DRAGON' (red), 'JAMAICAN HOT' (yellow and red), or 'YELLOW MUSHROOM'.

Notes

_____

_____

_____

more about peppers > >

< 69 >

'JUPITER' SWEET BELL

'SUPER CHILE' HOT PEPPER

'RED BEAUTY HYBRID' BELL

PURPLE SWEET PEPPER

How to grow

PLANTING: Pepper seeds require a high soil temperature to germinate, so in all but the hottest climates start them indoors 40 to 60 days before transplanting time, which is usually two weeks after the last frost. Or purchase transplants and set them out two weeks or so after the last frost.

Plant sweet and hot varieties as far apart as possible in the garden to prevent cross-pollination. In small gardens, sweet peppers that cross-pollinate with hot peppers will have a mildly tangy flavor.

< 70 >

CARE: Water transplants with a starter solution, such as Miracle-Gro Liquid Quick Start, to prevent transplant shock. Keep the soil consistently moist. ❶ Use a soaker hose during periods of drought or high heat. Spread a 1- to 2-inch layer of mulch around plants to help conserve moisture.

Prolonged temperatures below 60°F or above 90°F prevent fruit from forming. ❷ Be prepared to protect plants from such extremes with row covers and cloches to conserve warmth and with shade cloth to block the sun.

Peppers don't usually need staking, but large cultivars planted where they are exposed to strong winds may topple. Plant them in tomato cages.

PESTS: Knock off aphids with a strong spray from the garden hose; use a mild soap solution for heavy infestations. Handpick and destroy any beetles and caterpillars. If whole peppers rot, check for pepper maggots or corn earworms and destroy the entire plant if infested. Choose virus-resistant cultivars.

Harvest

Harvest often so the plants continue to produce fruits. ❸ Use scissors or pruners to cut the stems and avoid damaging the plants. Sweet peppers are fully ripe when they have changed from green to their final color, but you can pick them at any color. Harvest hot peppers anytime for fresh use, but leave them on the plants until they are fully ripe if you want to dry them.

To dry hot peppers, string them together by running a needle and thread through the tops near the caps and hang them in a cool, dry location with good air circulation.

Notes

_____

_____

_____

_____

< 71 >

'YUKON GOLD'

'PURPLE PERUVIAN'

POTATO PLANTS

'RED PONTIAC'

PLANTING GUIDE	
PLANT TYPE: Annual	
START FROM: Seed potatoes	
PLANTING DEPTH: 4–6"	
SPACING: 10–12"	
ROW SPACING: 24–36"	
DAYS TO HARVEST: 45–80	
FEATURES: Edible tubers; easy-to-grow, productive plants	

POTATOES are easy to grow and each plant should produce at least five potatoes. Potatoes stop producing new tubers when the soil warms up in summer. For that reason, it is important to choose varieties suited to your climate. In warm climates where the spring season is short, grow only fast-maturing varieties. In areas with long springs, plant both early and midseason potatoes. Small fingerling potatoes are fun to grow in any climate. They produce so many small tubers that you will get a good crop even where the potato season is short.

If your garden space is limited, you can grow potatoes aboveground in large boxes or bins.

< 72 >

Recommended cultivars

Early-maturing varieties ready to harvest in 55 to 75 days include yellow-fleshed 'ADORA', 'CHARLOTTE', and 'YUKON GOLD'; 'PURPLE PERUVIAN', a medium to large fingerling; and 'RED PONTIAC'. 'KENNEBEC' and 'IDA ROSE' are midseason varieties ready in 80 to 90 days. Late-maturing varieties include: 'BUTTE', 'GERMAN BUTTERBALL', and 'NOOKSACK'.

How to grow

PLANTING: Plant seed potatoes two to four weeks before the last frost date. Cut them into pieces, each with one or two eyes, or growing points, and some fleshy tuber attached. Use commercial seed potatoes; grocery store potatoes are usually treated to inhibit sprouting. Dry cut pieces overnight to help prevent rot. ❶ Plant the pieces cut side down in a 4-inch-deep trench in heavy soil or a 6-inch-deep trench in light soil. Cover with 2 to 4 inches of soil.

CARE: Keep soil consistently moist but not waterlogged until plants emerge. Then water only in periods of high heat or drought. Use a plant food that is higher in phosphorus and potassium than in nitrogen, which reduces plant vigor and can lead to disease. Hill soil around the base of the stems when plants are 6 to 8 inches tall, and repeat as they grow taller. When the plants reach full height, top the hills with mulch to conserve moisture and hold weeds down. Cover any tubers poking through the surface with more soil.

PESTS: To avoid blights, remove and destroy vegetative debris where pests may overwinter and plant potatoes in a new area each year. Pick Colorado potato beetles off plants and destroy them.

Harvest

For new potatoes, check plants about a week after they flower. Carefully loosen soil with a garden fork, then reach in to pull up usable size tubers. (Early varieties are the best new potatoes.) Harvest potatoes as needed. For potatoes you plan to store for winter use, leave tubers in the ground until plant tops die back, then dig up the plants and harvest the potatoes.

Notes

_____

_____

_____

< 73 >

RADISHES

'CHERRIETTE'
SALAD RADISH

'FRENCH BREAKFAST'

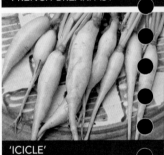

RADISHES   'ICICLE'

PLANTING GUIDE	
PLANT TYPE:	Annual
START FROM:	Seed
DEPTH:	½"
SPACING:	1–2"
ROW SPACING:	12"
DAYS TO HARVEST:	20–30
FEATURES:	Edible roots; fast-growing

RADISHES are often ready for harvest a month after planting. Plant these fast-growing, cool-season vegetables in early spring or fall in northern areas and in fall or winter in the South.

Salad radishes have small, round roots. They are available in red, white, and purple. French radishes grow into long cylinders with white tips and red shoulders. All-red and all-white types of French radishes are also available. Oriental daikon radishes produce huge carrot-shaped roots that can weigh several pounds. They are easy to grow in fall but often bolt when grown in spring.

< 74 >

Recommended cultivars

SALAD RADISHES: '**CHERRIETTE**', '**CHERRY BELLE**', and '**CHERRY BOMB**' are round, red types with a mild peppery flavor. '**ICICLE**' is a white, elongated radish.

FRENCH RADISHES: '**D'AVIGNON**' is a 3- to 4-inch tapered, cylindrical radish with a white tip. It is ready in only 21 days. '**FRENCH BREAKFAST**' is white with red shoulders.

ORIENTAL DAIKON: '**MIYASHIGE**' has long white roots banded with green at the top.

How to grow

PLANTING: Direct-sow radishes three to four weeks before the last spring frost and six weeks before the first fall frost in northern climates. Plant seeds in early autumn in hot climates. Sow small amounts of seed every few weeks so you can pick and eat radishes at their peak. Interplant them with slower-developing crops such as carrots, beans, and cucumbers.

CARE: ❶ Thin seedlings to 2 inches apart when they are 1 inch tall. Pull weeds by hand and keep the soil consistently moist.

PESTS: Choose cultivars labeled for disease resistance. To control clubroot, remove diseased plants and plant radishes in a new spot with well-drained soil every year. Remove and destroy leaves infected with leaf miners. Use floating row covers to discourage them, as well as cabbage maggot flies.

Harvest

❷ Radishes are the fastest crop in the garden. Pull them as soon as they're a usable size; if left in the ground too long they crack or become pithy. Trim off the tops and roots and scrub off the dirt under running water. Store radishes in the refrigerator for up to one month.

Notes

< 75 >

PARSNIPS

RUTABAGAS

RUTABAGAS | TURNIPS

PLANTING GUIDE	
PLANT TYPE: Annual	
START FROM: Seed	
DEPTH: ½"	
SPACING: Sow 2" apart; thin to 6–8" apart	
ROW SPACING: 12–24"	
DAYS TO HARVEST: 35–120, depending on the crop	
FEATURES: Edible roots	

ROOT CROPS, such as parsnips, turnips, and rutabagas, are the convenience food of the garden because they can be left in the ground for several weeks—or even months—until needed.

Parsnips are similar to carrots in shape and have a distinctive nutty flavor that mellows after cooking. Turnips have edible leaves and round roots. The leaves have a spicy flavor and the roots are peppery. These fast-maturing vegetables are ready for harvest in 35 to 75 days. Rutabagas have larger roots than turnips; the foliage is inedible. Rutabagas have a pleasing sweet, peppery flavor and are ready for harvest about 90 days after sowing.

< **76** >

Recommended cultivars

PARSNIPS: 'GLADIATOR' is sweet with good disease resistance. 'HARRIS MODEL' holds its white color after harvest.

TURNIPS: Grow 'HAKUREI' for sweet salad turnips, 'SHOGOIN' and 'TOKYO CROSS' for tender turnips and greens.

RUTABAGAS: 'JOAN' develops yellow-fleshed roots with purple tops.

How to grow

PLANTING: Direct-sow turnips and rutabagas four to six weeks before the last spring frost. Or sow in late summer for fall harvest in northern areas, in fall for winter harvest in southern regions. Direct-sow parsnips two to three weeks before the last average frost date. Keep the seedbed moist until seedlings emerge.

CARE: When seedlings are 1 inch tall, thin to 6 to 8 inches apart. To avoid disturbing nearby plants, cut rather than pull the seedlings. Feed root crops with a soluble high-potassium plant food once a month. ❶ Mulch to keep roots cool and summer and to protect plants over winter.

PESTS: Crop rotation helps control blights and molds. Use floating row covers to protect young plants from leafhoppers.

Harvest

PARSNIPS: After frost, dig roots all at once. Or mulch plants with 1 foot of straw to keep soil from freezing; harvest as needed through winter. Chilly soil brings out sweetness in parsnips and improves their texture.

TURNIPS: Harvest turnip greens by pulling individual leaves, or cutting them 1 inch above the crowns. Water plants after harvesting greens; they will quickly produce a flush of new leaves. ❷ Dig or pull roots when they are about 3 inches across. Harvest roots before temperatures drop below 25°F; they split and become woody after a hard freeze.

RUTABAGAS: Chilling improves flavor, so harvest after several frosts. In early winter trim the tops of remaining plants, mulch with 1 foot of straw, and continue harvesting during winter.

Notes

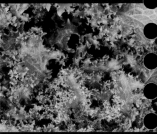

CURLY ENDIVE

ARUGULA

SALAD GREENS

'MIZUNA' AND ENDIVE

PLANTING GUIDE	
PLANT TYPE: Annual	
START FROM: Seed	
DEPTH: ¼"	
SPACING: Sow 1" apart; thin to 8–12" apart	
ROW SPACING: 12–24"	
DAYS TO HARVEST: 30–40	
FEATURES: Edible leaves	

SALAD GREENS are easy-to-grow, cool-season crops. They include arugula, endive, mustard, and other spring greens. Arugula is expensive at the grocery but easy to grow. Also known as roquette or rocket, it has a delicious, rich, full-bodied flavor. Endive looks and is planted like leaf lettuce in spring and fall, but it is more cold tolerant. Its flavor is sharp and peppery to almost bitter. Mustards are large, ornamental leafy vegetables with peppery flavor.

A good way to get to know salad greens without buying lots of different seed is to try a mesclun seed blend. Depending on the plants included in the mix, mesclun can be mild, spicy, or bitter.

< 78 >

Recommended cultivars

ARUGULA: 'ASTRO' and 'RUNWAY' are two early, vigorous varieties.

ENDIVE: 'GALIA' is a trouble-free variety with finely cut or curly leaves.

MUSTARD: 'MIZUNA' is an oriental mustard with long feathery leaves. 'RED GIANT' and 'OSAKA PURPLE' are colorful varieties.

How to grow

PLANTING: ❶ Direct-sow salad greens four to six weeks before the last frost. Plant every two weeks for continuous harvest. For fall crops, sow in midsummer in northern regions, late summer to fall in southern areas. ❷ Grow in cold frames for winter harvest.

CARE: Thin seedlings to 8 to 12 inches apart when plants are 3 to 4 inches tall. Water during dry periods. Mulch lightly to suppress weeds; protect plants from intense summer sun with a shade cloth suspended over them with stakes or hoops.

PESTS: Use floating row covers to protect plants from beetles.

Harvest

❸ When arugula and mesclun leaves are about 3 inches long, harvest by cutting handfuls of leaves 1 to 2 inches above the soil surface. Water after harvesting to help plants quickly produce a second crop.

Harvest endive like arugula and mesclun or wait until leaves form a large, loose head with a white to light green heart. Gardeners often blanch mature endive for two weeks before harvest. To blanch, tie outer leaves into a bundle over the hearts; hold it in place with string or a rubber band.

Notes

_____

_____

_____

_____

< **79** >

'OLYMPIA'

'MELODY'

'BLOOMSDALE LONGSTANDING'

SPINACH

PLANTING GUIDE	
PLANT TYPE: Annual	
START FROM: Seed	
DEPTH: ½"	
SPACING: Sow 1"; thin to 6–9"	
ROW SPACING: 12–18"	
DAYS TO HARVEST: 35–50	
FEATURES: Edible leaves	

SPINACH is packed with nutrients and turns everyday salads into treats. A cool-season plant, spinach can take temperatures as low as 10 to 20°F. Plant it early for a bountiful spring and early summer crop.

Smooth-leaf spinach varieties are best grown in spring after the chance of snow and ice has passed. Many smooth-leaf varieties are slow to bolt; they produce into summer. Semisavoyed varieties have leaves that are slightly crinkled. They also have thicker leaves and produce well in spring or fall. Savoyed spinach has thick, heavily crinkled leaves. It holds up well to winter weather and makes an outstanding fall and winter crop.

< 80 >

Recommended cultivars

SMOOTH-LEAF: 'SPACE' produces tender, thin leaves on upright stems. **'OLYMPIA'** is best grown in early spring. **'WHALE'** is mildew and bolt resistant.

SEMISAVOYED: 'TYEE' and **'MELODY'** are slow to bolt and have slightly crinkled leaves.

SAVOYED: 'BLOOMSDALE LONGSTANDING' has thick, heavily crinkled leaves.

How to grow

PLANTING: ❶ Direct-sow spinach four to six weeks before the last spring frost date in northern climates and in late winter in southern regions. Make successive sowings of spinach every few weeks to extend the harvest until late spring. In warmer weather, plant slow-to-bolt cultivars.

CARE: Thin seedlings to 6 inches apart when they reach 3 inches in height. Thin as they grow to provide good air circulation around plants, which helps prevent rust diseases. Keep soil consistently moist and mulch to cool roots. Water in the morning so that plants have time to dry.

PESTS: ❷ Cover young plants with floating row covers to protect them from leaf miners and flea beetles. Aphids can be knocked off by a strong spray from the garden hose. Handpick and destroy caterpillars. Choose cultivars that are resistant to downy mildew and mosaic virus to avoid those diseases.

Harvest

❸ Begin harvesting when plants are 6 inches tall. If you take two to three leaves per plant, you can harvest from each plant once every 10 days.

Notes

_____

_____

_____

_____

< 81 >

SUMMER SQUASH

ACORN WINTER SQUASH

BUTTERNUT AND OTHER WINTER SQUASHES

PUMPKIN

PLANTING GUIDE	
PLANT TYPE: Annual	
START FROM: Seed or transplants	
DEPTH: ¾–1"	
SPACING: 18–36"	
ROW SPACING: 72–96"	
DAYS TO HARVEST: 45–120	
FEATURES: Edible fruits	

PUMPKINS AND SQUASH provide fall beauty as well as healthful fruits. Their vigorous vines grow quickly and need as much as 25 square feet to sprawl. For small gardens, look for cultivars that have a compact, bushy habit.

Two groups of vegetables go by the name of squash. Summer squash—including zucchini, Lebanese, pattypan, crookneck, and straightneck—have soft skin. Winter squash—including acorn, butternut, buttercup, hubbard, and pumpkins—have hard, thick rinds, making them suitable for long-term storage.

< 82 >

Recommended cultivars

Hundreds of squash and pumpkin varieties are available. Choose ones suited for your climate.

How to grow

PLANTING: Direct-sow seed two to three weeks after the last spring frost date. Plant in rows or in hills of five to seven seeds. In short-season areas, start seeds indoors four weeks before the last frost date. Move seeds to the garden after the last frost date.

CARE: Squash and pumpkins have high moisture and nutrient requirements. Feed twice a month with water-soluble plant food. Maintain consistently moist but not waterlogged soil. Moisture-stressed plants are more susceptible to insects and diseases and have lower yields. ❶ Because the fruit ripens on the ground, slip a piece of cardboard or another barrier underneath it to prevent rot.

PESTS: ❷ Squash bugs are the most significant pests. Winter squashes are especially susceptible to them. Choose resistant cultivars. Adult squash bugs are difficult to eradicate, so treat plants with Ortho Bug-B-Gon Garden & Landscape Insect Killer when you first see the nymphs. Time sprays carefully to avoid killing pollinators. Crop rotation can also help control insects.

Diseases affecting squash and pumpkins include: fusarium wilt, anthracnose, rots, leaf spots, gummy stem blight, and powdery mildew.

Harvest

Summer squash tastes best when picked small—zucchinis, crooknecks, and straightnecks at about 6 inches long and pattypans at about 3 inches across. Harvest daily when plants are at the height of production.

Winter squash and pumpkins need to mature on the plants until the vines begin to turn yellow and die back; they will not ripen further once picked and do not develop flavor if picked early.

Notes

< 83 >

PLANTING GUIDE

PLANT TYPE: Annual vine

START FROM: Rooted slips

DEPTH: ½–1"

SPACING: 12"

ROW SPACING: 30–36"

DAYS TO HARVEST: 90–120

FEATURES: Edible tubers

SWEET POTATOES thrive where warm weather lasts at least three months. New early cultivars make it easy to grow sweet potatoes in cool climates. Despite their name sweet potatoes are not potatoes. The vining plants form a lovely green ground cover, and each one produces four or more sweet tubers.

< 84 >

Recommended cultivars

'GEORGIA JET' is a good choice for areas with short summers. 'ALL GOLD' has moist salmon-colored flesh and resists stem rot. Bush types, such as 'VARDAMAN' and 'PORTO RICO', do well in small gardens and in containers.

How to grow

PLANTING: Grow sweet potatoes from slips, which are 6-inch-long rooted stems. Purchase disease-free slips in late spring or grow your own by soaking the ends of sweet potatoes in a jar of water on a windowsill. Each potato will produce two to four leafy stems with a few stringy roots. About three to four weeks after the last frost and when slips are 4 to 6 inches long, break off the slips and plant them in the garden. Water them with a starter solution.

CARE: Keep soil consistently moist to promote plant growth and prevent cracked tubers. If soil is poor, feed plants once with a low-nitrogen plant food.

PESTS: To prevent soilborne diseases, avoid planting sweet potatoes in the same place more than once every three or four years, and buy certified disease-free slips. Use row covers to protect plants from flea beetles and cutworms. Overwatering may attract root weevils.

Harvest

1 Harvest after plants have been nipped by frost. **2** Cut back the plants, **3** then dig tubers carefully, loosening the soil with a garden fork. Cure the tubers for two to three weeks in a warm, humid area. Wrap cured tubers in newspaper and store in a warm (55°F to 60°F), dry location; chilling injures sweet potatoes.

Notes

< 85 >

CHERRY TOMATOES

PLUM TOMATOES

INDETERMINATE TOMATOES

PATIO TOMATOES

PLANTING GUIDE	
PLANT TYPE: Annual	
START FROM: Seed or transplants	
DEPTH: ½"	
SPACING: 24–36"	
ROW SPACING: 36–72"	
DAYS TO HARVEST: 50–80	
FEATURES: Edible fruit	

TOMATOES come in diverse sizes, shapes, and colors as well as growing habits. You can purchase plum, cherry, grape, pear, or beefsteak types in red, yellow, peach, black, green, or variegated colors.

Successfully growing tomatoes is simple: Choose disease-resistant varieties suited to your climate and do everything you can to help the plants grow steadily and without interruption.

< 86 >

Recommended cultivars

There are three types of tomatoes: determinate, vigorous determinate, and indeterminate.

DETERMINATE tomatoes, sometimes called dwarf varieties, grow into bushy plants that need no support and develop clusters of blossoms and fruit at the stem tips. They mature early and ripen within one to two weeks, so they are ideal for canning or freezing and for growing in short-season areas. Generally, the fruit ripens over a concentrated period of time, usually three weeks, then the plants die. 'TINY TIM' is a compact plant suitable for containers. 'BUSH EARLY GIRL' is a small, disease-resistant plant that bears large fruit. 'CELEBRITY' is a disease-resistant midseason cultivar with 7- to 8-ounce fruits. 'SHADY LADY' is popular in hot climates. 'SUPER BUSH' bears large, meaty fruit all season but is only 3 feet tall and wide and requires no stakes or cages. 'ROMA' and 'LaROMA' have rich, meaty, almost seedless fruits on compact, disease-resistant vines. 'WINDOWBOX ROMA' is good for growing in containers.

VIGOROUS DETERMINATE tomatoes produce a heavy crop all at once, but they do not die afterward. If you prune them back and fertilize them in midsummer after harvest, vigorous determinates produce a light second crop. They are increasingly popular as double-crop tomatoes, especially in warm climates. 'HUSKY GOLD' is a good yellow-fruiting cultivar.

INDETERMINATE tomatoes produce a summerlong stream of flowers and fruit. The tall, lanky plants require support from stakes, a trellis, or wire cages. Their fruit usually has excellent flavor, and plants remain productive until frost, insects, or diseases kill them. 'GRAPE' is a small, sweet, early, disease-resistant cultivar. 'JOLLY' bears extra-sweet fruits whose tips are pointed like peaches. 'EARLY GIRL' is a popular early slicing tomato that adapts well to almost any climate and is disease resistant. 'SIOUX' is an heirloom variety with exceptional flavor. 'BRANDYWINE' and 'GERMAN JOHNSON' are hybrid heirloom beefsteak varieties with very large dark pink fruit often weighing a pound or more apiece.

Notes

more about tomatoes >>

BEEFSTEAK-TYPE TOMATO

YELLOW PEAR TOMATO

'BRANDYWINE' HEIRLOOM TOMATO   'SUBARCTIC PLENTY'

How to grow

PLANTING: You'll harvest tomatoes sooner by starting with transplants, which you can buy transplants or grow yourself. Sow seeds indoors 6 to 10 weeks before the last frost date. Put the pots in a warm (75°F to 85°F), spot where you can set up grow-lights. Illuminate the seedlings for 12 hours each day, raising the lamps every few days so that they are 3 inches above the tops of the plants.

Plant seedlings in the garden after the last frost date has passed. Dig a deep hole or a trench long enough that you can bury the stem. Place a handful of well-rotted compost in the bottom of the hole or trench, ❶ then set the plant in it. Cover stem and roots with soil, water thoroughly, and apply a starter plant solution. ❷ Stake the plants or set cages over

< 88 >

them now to avoid injuring roots later. Staking elevates foliage so air circulates around it and holds the fruits off the ground, which increases yield. The mesh of cages should be large enough to reach through for harvest. Stakes should be at least 8 feet tall, 1 inch around, and made of sturdy wood or metal. Begin tying stems to the stakes with strips of soft cloth or garden twine when their tips droop.

CARE: Tomatoes need plenty of water to develop juicy fruits and resist disease. Water regularly and apply organic mulch to conserve soil moisture and control weeds. Feed with a water-soluble plant food such as Miracle-Gro Water Soluble Tomato Plant Food, following package directions.

PESTS: The most common diseases are anthracnose, early blight, septoria leaf spot, tobacco mosaic virus, fusarium wilt, and verticillium wilt. Look for disease-resistant varieties. Tomatoes suffer from numerous physiological disorders caused by environmental stress. Moisture extremes cause blossom-end rot. Skin cracking happens when hot rainy periods follow dry spells. Temperature extremes lead to blossom drop. Sunscald results from overexposure to the sun on one side of the fruit.

Handpick and destroy Japanese beetles or hornworms. Control fruitworms and stinkbugs with a labeled insecticide.

Harvest

Begin picking tomatoes when they reach full size and color. Tomatoes will continue ripening off the plant, even in the dark. The pigments that give fruits their distinctive color do not develop well in high temperatures, so tomatoes harvested during midsummer may be more yellow than when picked in cooler weather.

Pick any fruits remaining on the vine at the first predicted autumn frost. Fruits that have a hint of yellow often continue to ripen if held in a dark, warm location. Store them in single layers between sheets of newspaper.

Notes

'YELLOW DOLL'

ICEBOX WATERMELON

WATERMELON

'DEUCE OF HEARTS'

PLANTING GUIDE	
PLANT TYPE: Annual vine	
START FROM: Seed or transplants	
DEPTH: ¼"	
SPACING: Sow 12" apart; thin to 36"	
ROW SPACING: 72–96"	
DAYS TO HARVEST: 70–100	
FEATURES: Edible fruit	

WATERMELONS that grow in the typical large oblong shape require a long, hot growing season. Smaller icebox melons, with fruit weighing 10 pounds or less, ripen in as few as 80 days of warm temperatures. Icebox melon vines can grow 10 to 15 feet long and require a space at least 8 feet wide and 12 feet long for five plants. It takes a plot twice that size to grow large-fruited watermelon.

Watermelons are available in red-, yellow-, and orange-fleshed cultivars. There are seedless varieties too. They have a long growing season and are best for hot climates.

< 90 >

Recommended cultivars

'FIESTA', 'REGENCY', and 'SANGRIA' are striped dark green melons weighing 20 to 25 pounds. 'SUGAR BUSH', 'SUGAR BABY', and yellow-fleshed 'YELLOW DOLL' are compact vines with small melons that easily fit in the refrigerator. 'DEUCE OF HEARTS' is compact and seedless.

How to grow

PLANTING: Direct-sow seeds in southern regions after the last frost date. Sow six seeds in a hill 3 inches tall and 12 inches in diameter. ❶ In cool climates, start seeds indoors three weeks before the last frost date. Sow seeds in peat pots or in flats of potting soil; transplant seedlings into the garden at least two weeks after the last frost.

CARE: Thin direct-sown seedlings to four plants per hill after the first set of true leaves appears, then to one or two plants when vines are 12 to 24 inches long. Hand weed to avoid damaging vines. Watermelons are heavy feeders; use plant food, such as Miracle-Gro Water Soluble All Purpose, throughout the growing season and Miracle-Gro Shake 'n Feed Continuous Release All Purpose at planting. Place cardboard squares under ripening fruits to protect them from rot and insects.

PESTS: Cover plants with floating row covers to discourage cucumber beetles and aphids. Remove the fabric when flowers bloom. Wash off aphids with a mild soap solution.

Scrape off squash bug nymphs (red dots on the undersides of leaves); treat with insecticide if the infestation is heavy.

To prevent the spread of disease, avoid wetting leaves and handling wet plants. Plant in a new area every year.

Harvest

Watermelons are ready to harvest when the green stem and tendrils near the top of the melon dry out and turn brown. The underside of the fruit of some cultivars turns from white to yellow when ripe. Melons do not ripen off the vine.

Notes

MORE GREAT VEGETABLES

Here are nine more easy-to-grow plants for your vegetable garden. Although they are less common than ever-popular tomatoes, beans, and corn, these unique vegetables boast abundant produce with fresh-from-the-garden flavor.

Plant	Features	Days to harvest
Collards	Edible leaves	70–85
Edamame	Vegetable soybean; edible beans	80–90
Ginger	Edible root	100–120
Horseradish	Edible root	180–240
Jerusalem artichoke	Edible root; attractive flowers	120–150
Kohlrabi	Edible stem	50–75
Rhubarb	Edible leaf stalks	2 years after planting; then harvest for 8 to 10 weeks each spring
Sunflower	Edible seeds	80–110
Tomatillo	Edible fruits	100–120

INDEX

< 92 >

This map of climate zones helps you select plants for your garden that will survive a typical winter in your region. The United States Department of Agriculture (USDA) developed the map, basing the zones on the lowest recorded temperatures across North America. Zone 1 is the coldest area and Zone 11 is the warmest.

Plants are classified by the coldest temperature and zone they can endure. For example, plants hardy to Zone 6 survive where winter temperatures drop to −10° F. Those hardy to Zone 8 die long before it's that cold. These plants may grow in colder regions but must be replaced each year. Plants rated for a range of hardiness zones can usually survive winter in the coldest region as well as tolerate the summer heat of the warmest one.

To find your hardiness zone, note the approximate location of your community on the map, then match the color band marking that area to the key.

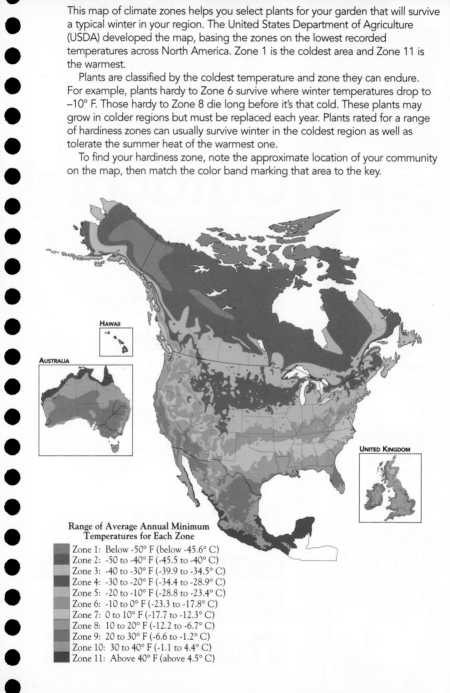

Range of Average Annual Minimum Temperatures for Each Zone

Zone 1: Below -50° F (below -45.6° C)
Zone 2: -50 to -40° F (-45.5 to -40° C)
Zone 3: -40 to -30° F (-39.9 to -34.5° C)
Zone 4: -30 to -20° F (-34.4 to -28.9° C)
Zone 5: -20 to -10° F (-28.8 to -23.4° C)
Zone 6: -10 to 0° F (-23.3 to -17.8° C)
Zone 7: 0 to 10° F (-17.7 to -12.3° C)
Zone 8: 10 to 20° F (-12.2 to -6.7° C)
Zone 9: 20 to 30° F (-6.6 to -1.2° C)
Zone 10: 30 to 40° F (-1.1 to 4.4° C)
Zone 11: Above 40° F (above 4.5° C)